REBEL

UNTETHERED

It's In Your Blood to Fight

JAMES S. ZAKARIA

Copyright 2020 - REBEL UNTETHERED

- It's In Your Blood to Fight - by James S. Zakaria

All rights reserved.

Published by Hasfeld X Publishing.

Dedicated to my family and the thought leaders
who have influenced me the most

The Courageous James Altucher, the Articulate Jordan Peterson, the Adventurous Mark Manson, the Charming Jay Shetty, the Eloquent Robin Sharma, the Daring Brene Brown, the Wise Depak Chopra, the Admirable Malcolm Gladwell, the Original Seth Godin, the Agreeable Lewis Howes, the Genuine Don Miguel Ruiz, the Hilarious Jen Sincero, the Dynamic Patrick Bet-David, the Compassionate Marie Forleo, the Conscientious Vishen Lakhiani, the Impressive Ryan Holiday, the Brilliant Robert Greene, the Passionate Eric Thomas, the Insightful Gary John Bishop, the Captivating Elizabeth Gilbert, the Extraordinary Tony Robbins, and the Charismatic Tom Bilyeu. With a special thanks to the Amazing Gretchen Rubin.

Contents

PREFACE

Call to Arms

Every chapter in here is one form of rebellion against the past or defiance of the average. For example, after a week of writers' hell, I ultimately jammed this three-page introduction, in all it's mediocrity, into 'Rebel, Untethered' to force its completion. But that's what we do—Modern 21st-century rebels do not fight civil wars or start violent revolutions. We revolt through action and creation against society's norms, values, and traditions by defying expectations and doing things our way.

Rebels fight back against the orders and wishes of others, and, what is worse, we inexplicably battle against our own desires, goals, and projects as well. That is the issue here; radicals like myself tend to frustrate, self-sabotage, self-destruct and go to war against themselves in our quest for a good life.

Hardwired in early childhood, the tendency to push back against authority does not come from parenting styles, gender, religion,

"

careers, aging, or the country they live in. Rebel's revolt against inner and outer obligations because they must. I would not wish this rebel character on anyone. It is more of a curse than a blessing for the seventeen percent of adults troubled with this personality type, although many triumphant rebels would disagree with such a bold statement.

Still, confused? Do you know any adults who won't do what they are told despite repeated instruction? Do they say the following "You can't make me? I do what I want. When I feel like it. Rules are made to be broken. You are not the boss of me?" Do you know people who are artists, entrepreneurs, inventors who seem to do things in private, in their own time, in their particular way? Those are the rebels I speak of!

Rebels are in great danger of failure. Friends and family cannot shame a rebel into doing useful jobs that could alter them into winners. Squeezing our minds with the simple guilting of obligation is an exercise in futility. One must plunge in a metaphorical knife and twist wisely until it hurts enough for rebels to recoil from childhood trauma & comply with orders.

On the other hand, Rebels' contrarian nature can make them easy to manipulate. Tell them to do something, and they will do the opposite even if life-threatening. Praise them, and they might quit.

Rewards can backfire. Pushing creates resistance. Innovative organizations like criminal gangs, advertisers and con artists can easily tap into the need to rebel, leading radicals astray.

This is not a small issue! Born into a society where the vast majority are indoctrinated and taught to fit into a land full of rules, norms, and institutions, rebels are the last holdouts. This goes far beyond teenage rebellion and finding our place as young adults. There is some kind of primitive wildness deep inside a rebel that yearns for freedom from work, parental obligations, time clocks, and the drudgery of life.

Radicals confound and frustrate teachers, parents, and bosses who understand the need for law and order establishments. This divide in personality traits sets up countless conflicts as leaders seek to herd followers into groupings while rebels fight to break free. Radicals are told they are stupid, foolish, lazy, incompetent because they won't get with the program. Sometimes, they are rewarded with mediocre employment & postings, social disapproval, and even bullying, imprisonment, and execution.

Not that it isn't our fault. We were given the program, told the rules, and disobeyed orders anyway. As responsible adults, we must take the blame on ourselves. We must also endeavor to search for a solution that meets our needs and the community we belong to.

Based on the research of Gretchen Rubin, and as outlined in her fantastic book "The Four Tendencies," hundreds of thousands of online users were surveyed, and she found that humans fall into one of four groups or tendencies: Upholders, Obligers, Questioners, and Rebels. The other three personalities are more traditionalists and met at least one of two expectations: inner and outer expectations.

Rebels resist both inner presumptions from themselves and outer assumptions from others, and this instability makes for more difficult lives of quiet desperation. Personal biases aside, I believe Rebels are at the most elevated risk of either becoming a spectacular success or exploding into a wreckage of substance addiction, depression, and bitterness.

Make no mistake, you or someone you know could be in peril of living a failed and discontented life because we are fighting to live an existence that is as uncomfortable as ill-fitting clothing.

If you care about the rebels in your life or are one yourself, this book could be a revelation, a great boon that could reorient a lost soul back onto their prescribed path.

Most rebels are without a cause, they must discover compulsive rule-breaking is in their DNA, so they can call a peace accord on their internal struggle to find themselves. It's a terrible thing to not know who you really are, why you behave in specific ways, or the heights you are capable of. Millions genuinely believe their behavior is a deficit of character rather than a personality trait acquired in infancy. There are no schools for rebels, other than art & drama, but there should be!

Countless would-be-warriors wander lost in a society lacking knowledge of what to make of their tendency to rebel or how to adapt to others' needs. People must suffer great tragedies in their lives but not appreciating who they are or their purpose is a needless one.

Those who know us well realize that rebels can become the administrators of our own negativity, cynicism & depravity after years of struggle & failure. Without guidance, we will torture ourselves with endless worrying and imprison ourselves inside jail cells of our own making with self-destructive behaviors.

You value the importance of knowing yourself through reading, and those with rebellious traits would also appreciate gaining critical pieces of wisdom about themselves.

Rebels are among society's best weapons to reduce corruption, criminality, and waste. We appreciate authenticity and honesty, so we fight to uncover the truth as journalists, artists, and entrepreneurs. Not all famous people are of the rebel tendency, but all notable names in history have some shade of rebellion and descent in their actions.

Many radicals are so passionate and focused on enormous dreams, which require extensive exploration and experimentation, that all the mundane, routine aspects of their lives are chaotic and disorganized. This causes unnecessary misery for them and their families. As peaceful revolutionaries of this time, we are so messy & scattered that we need your guidance and assistance to manage our affairs while we make right all that is wrong.

There is a war of ideologies brewing that threatens to turn the planet into tens or hundreds of thousands of digital feudalistic classes (don't ask, that's another possible book). Patriots who advocate for religious, political, and economic freedoms absolutely need rebels in their camps to fight on their behalf, whatever may transpire.

Rebels who accept themselves as such are more likely to quell the conflict within and turn it outward. Instead of engaging in silly arguments and disputes, they can use this energy to advocate for causes more significant than themselves with guidance and wisdom.

Should you agree that there is something here, please don't order or pressure the rebels in your life to pick up this title. They hate being directed into corners or receiving intimations that they must change their ways. Maybe suggest that this simple book has a few interesting concepts that could be beneficial for whatever purpose or cause they are working on?

If you are curious about which of the four personality tendencies you belong to or want to confirm whether you are a genuine rebel at heart, why not try out Ms. Rubins' quiz? at: **happiercast.com/quiz** (no affiliation to this writer)

My last thought - Is it possible that acquiring one new idea can transform a rebel's life? I believe so, that's why I write...

CHAPTER 1

Proclamation of Untethered Rebels

A. I Will No Longer Revolt against Myself

- I am a rebel! I will not sin against myself by betraying my nature. Rebelling against the rules is what I do. I detest being told what to do and when I should do it with every fiber of my being. Others think there is something wrong with me because they can't imagine why anyone would want to fight against the global economy's technical marvel that provides so much plastic materialism & hedonistic pleasure? But I must rebel. It's in my nature to do so.

- We are peaceful revolutionaries of modern times. I will forsake violence and destruction on wrongdoers as a measure of last resort, for if I willfully harm others in the name of transformation, I become the tyrant I fought against. Instead, we shall determine how all institutions of evil, criminality, and injustice can be reassembled through words, kindness, and assistance rather than force and military might.

- I get to determine the criteria for success, no one else. I disavow notions that my net worth is the foundation for my self-worth. I am greater than my job title, bank account, & the car I drive. Whether a pilot, a hitchhiker, a surgeon, a barista, an executive, or a salesperson, only I know whether I am gratified and satisfied with my choices in life.

- If my path forces me to choose between being financially wealthy and being true to myself, I select authenticity over gold with ease. No martyr, when my purpose affords me the bounty of riches and acclaim, I will savor life freely, without guilt or reservation.

- When commitments for silly things and trivialities interfere with my happiness, I shall walk away. I am not persuaded by the obligations, guilt, manners, norms, and conformity that strain society's sorrow. I make my own rules, and I have to stand by them to seize my personal freedom away from the greedy arms of the maleficent and manipulative.

- I not only fight the establishment's rules; I rebel against myself. Even if I make plans or set a schedule for myself, I would not do it if it did not feel right. Other personalities feel like they must follow the rules, obey parents, and authorities in what they say, limiting their options. My rebellious nature allows me to break free of these norms and be almost anything I want to be.

- As the artisans, musicians, storytellers, advocates, craftspersons, inventors, and revolutionaries, we are society's lightning rod that demolishes ignorance, forces exchange, and ignites transformation. I will no longer stay in silence. Keeping my thoughts, art, and desires to myself may result in tight shoulders, stiff movements, frowning, and griping until I explode in rage or collapse in depression. Rebels must express themselves or shrink into nothingness.

B. I Will No Longer Be Moved By Lies & Manipulation

- I am a rebel. I have been misled countlessly about who I am and who I should be. These ignorant lies have ultimately sent me in the wrong direction, away from the person I was meant to be, and into the mass of mediocrity. It is a sin to go against myself, so I shall return in God's favor by the grace of the universe.

- I disavow status-seeking & social climbing as an awful game with few winners and scores of losers. Rebels desire to share happiness and responsibilities more justly because a hundred small stars can outshine one giant sun if love lines them up in the right direction.

- Not all of us can become ballerinas, firefighters, astronauts, and princesses. With no acclaim from journalists and no mention in any history books, we, the workers, shall do our part to serve. Neither fame, fortune, nor popularity will sustain my happiness should I go against my true nature. The wealthy and powerful can be as ignorant, foolish, weak, and reckless as the infirm and destitute in their greed for immortality.

- There is no fulfillment in joining those who talk of their dreams but don't do anything about it. I will not project my aspirations to conform with my admirers' frustrations and instead turn my passions into reality despite my paralyzing fears. I will take action; surrender of my goals goes against my more thoughtful nature.

- I will walk through the fog of misinformation, insufficient data, and unlimited choices, most of which are wild impositions on my consciousness. My mind is clouded with conflicting rules of conduct imposed by people who desire quick and easy solutions that cause heartache for billions.

They may push or encourage me to join their way of thinking, but my self-awareness is superior to what they can imagine. I am a rebel.

C. I Will Not Conform If Doing So Betrays My Purpose

- I am a rebel. Your judgment of me is as likely to be mistaken as it is right. If you notice something and describe it the way you perceive it, the odds say that you will be wildly inaccurate in your report. How can you? You are guessing based on your personal and limited history of exposure to unfamiliar people who are figments of your creative mind. I know me, and you do not!

- I fight for happiness, wealth, freedom, peace, and joy for all. What do you fight for? Does your desire for stability, safety, conformity, and confidence make you my enemy? If it is not in your nature to rebel from a marketplace that rewards few and enslaves many, stand aside. Please do not bar those who wish to enact the vision of a better tomorrow. Your mind will provide you a logical justification for rejecting this opportunity because your fears overwhelm your hopes.

- I will seek to reinforce positive thinking and optimism, but I will not endeavor to drive my pessimism, hatred, jealousy, laziness, and sadness undercover to hide in the depths of my soul. I shall inescapably become angry and upset during battles for my cause; thus, my rage anchors my passions to the vessel that is my heart. I will step away from the inauthenticity and falsities of modern society, no matter the damage, because it commands the suppression of what makes me real.

- My life will be slovenly until the exalted end because seeking the truth requires unpacking boxes and laying all the contents all over the floor. I will not try to mislabel others, prejudge them, put them in unfair containers to organize this chaos in my head. I must explore the world's secrets, for few are willing to step into a fog of lies to retrieve harsh truths. Despite the consequences, I remain a rebel.

D. I Will Not Fall Into Failure & Depression

- I am a rebel. I gain power by expressing my anxieties and worries to a sympathetic ear. I will not continue to dwell on the hurt and anguish caused by others, the disappointments, the regrets. When feelings of shame and guilt surface about what I did or did not do, I will acknowledge my culpability and then release that guilt. I did not know any better and may absolve myself of my part or remain in sin.

- Despite my hesitation, I shall forgive those who have wronged me in the past. I pardon my critics, not to enlarge a feeling of moral superiority but to clear the way to forgive myself. For if I do not, I will probably replay loud arguments and abusive confrontations in my mind like a never-ending torture program. My unfortunate past is kept alive through memories, and the spirit of forgiveness shall erase their power over me.

- I will not allow depression, worry, and anxiety assigned by my past to steal energy from my present. I will strive to fashion senseless anger from false thoughts into fertile ventures. Rather than rain down destruction on my world, I will employ gratitude exercises to appreciate all that I have and those who support me. Gratitude furnishes me with a newly acquired explosion of consciousness to recognize the beautiful world around me with clarity.

- I shed my glum past like a pack mule drops its burden. I reject this molten anger because I do not wish to become an angry person. When I hate far too many people, I fear I will transform into a hateful person who seeks to annihilate rather than build the world I favor. I need a vast and expansive reason for being that requires all my energy and devotion, and living my new identity gives me the required structure to silence the cacophony of my mind.

E. I Will Overcome My Flaws & Restore My Strengths.

- I am a rebel. It's challenging for me to change my behaviors without the outside influence of non-rebels. We dislike routines, mundane, and repetitive tasks because our minds have a low tolerance for boredom. Yet successful people assert that daily trudging through the muck of work is the key to winning. I must take into confidence allies with strengths I lack, ask for assistance, and accept others' dependence with a peaceful heart.

- I resolve not to worry about small things (and most situations are more trivial than we believe.) My pessimistic ruminations are a lack of confidence in myself to handle new challenges. To expand my freedom & fulfillment, I may have to perform actions that strike fear into the bravest of souls before gaining the confidence I desire. Should I crave to diminish my worries and acquire stronger self-confidence, I must do what must be done, no matter how terrified I feel.

- It is in my nature to fight against injustice, dishonesty, and the mistreatment of the powerless. Sometimes I will be as loud as thunder in a rainstorm; on other occasions, I will be like a whisper in the breeze. Ordinary people are afraid to speak against authority because they are chained by conformity thinking, traditions, and docility to customs that do not constrain me. For me, to do nothing would be sinful.

- Knowing that this automatic response to avoid following society's customs and my own personal rules explains why I fit the rebel tendency. I struggle to meet appointments, pay bills on time, and avoid obligations - for this, my reputation is besmirched, my credit damaged, and my name sullied. I resolve to try to change my ways, so I call myself a 'Reluctant Rebel.'

F. I Accept The Disagreeable Struggle Of My Humble Cause.

- I am a rebel. At the risk of my sanity and balance, I chose a difficult life as someone who fights against traditions and standards. Despite delicious temptations that magnetize the crowds, it is not my purpose to live a 9-5, manicured lawn, cocktail party type of existence. I reject future attempts to fit in. Conformity is a more comfortable choice, but my spirit vehemently protests, wearing chains that slowly strangle my independence.

- I will fight for what I believe in, as did General George Washington during the American Revolutionary War. Stars don't just lead nations to victory, free the oppressed, or establish democracies. We volunteer for causes, tutor children, fight fires, designate drive, rescue cats, cook and clean, and offer a compassionate ear. We do what is right when it is called for. We fight unabashedly for those who need help because it is in us to contribute.

- I will not join in with snobs who smugly watched other rebels struggle with their inner demons and relished in their failures. I will not laugh and gossip with false friends about strangers assumed beneath them. Why would I place commensurate obstacles that barred my path in the door of potential allies? Revolutionaries do not confront, argue, or show off when we achieve success - to do so is to fall into shallow impulses we abhor.

- To live an apathetic, futile life is to live a lie because I am lying to myself that death is not coming. I will not participate in the mass delusion that nothing matters or that my contribution has little value to the universe. I shall not betray my worth by killing my abilities solely on money making. When I leave it all on the table and have nothing left to give, my departure is more significant because an empty life devoid of action will be swelled with thoughts of regrets and dying unhappily.

G. I Will Modify My Emotions Into Exponential Power

- I am a rebel. I must shut off the screaming, frightened part of my subconscious mind that blocks me from moving forward and stepping into a place where I have not been before. I will scorn my critics' voices because they are limited to merely judging this package's wrapping. They know not what is inside. I must move towards worthy goals or risk stagnating in a position where time will run out before I learn who I really am.

- If I fall off my correct path, my voice in my head will start to grumble and shout until it drives away the joy & contentment in my life. My restless thoughts will wake me up in the middle of the night and disrupt my meaningless actions. My soul will rumble in my body, my face a display of sullen scowls, my figure shall reveal a dispirited walk. My inner voice will whisper in the shower, "Why won't you listen to me? Why won't you be the person you were meant to be?"

- My actions allow me to release the passive, simmering, unexpressed rage inside. I will not join the millions walking around full of anger that they keep bottled up inside. They are furious because other people hurt them and their internal beliefs told them that they will be punished if they express that anger. They are irate because they are working hard, stuck, can't ask for help, and can't be themselves. I shall channel my anger into my work, and the results shall be immeasurable.

- I shall not impose my beliefs, ideology, or values onto others as a matter of debate or discussion - except in cases of the common good. Rebels are often boisterous and loud about politics, religion, and parenting when none of our business pertains to how conservatives should live. To ask for space to be ourselves, we must give what we want to others in return. I am a rebel, and we fight to do what is right, even if unpopular.

H. I Shall Release Myself From My Inner Conflict To Prepare For Greater Challenges.

- I am a rebel. I will not be afraid to make mistakes. My fear of errors prevents progress because the only way to become successful is to make blunders. When we tell ourselves not to worry through will power, we will fail within minutes because we ask our conscious minds not to do something our subconscious minds want. That is like telling a thief to guard the treasure.

- I will no longer remain in bondage by my regrets or risk never encountering the full richness of life. Should I fail to do so, as my seasons spin to a halt, my mind will be full of sorrows, of the friendships lost, the ample opportunities missed, the adventures never took. That is, if I do not grab hold of this tree of enlightenment and shake it vigorously until all its fruits rain down for my sustenance.

- I will fight my impulse to hate opponents and critics because it damages relationships and separates me from potential friends. I will not stifle my resentment with indifference and boredom because being heartless is a failure to be loving. If the world is bountiful, hatred implies a significant loss that cannot be replaced, and I chose to believe I have the power to recover anything or any person I care about.

- My inner critic is going to sing in harmony with my decision to break away from the pack. Even if it means becoming far more successful than my friends and parents. Indeed if it means giving up some meaningless pleasures in life. Even if I suffer multiple episodes of rejection until I escape living under the thumb of oppressors. Rebels can't be half-pregnant. Either I am all in, or I am out completely.

- I am a rebel. It is my personal power to diminish hatred & anger because only I can decide how to respond to my feelings. Hostility and anger temporarily awaken me from my usual zombie-like state to the non-acceptance of the present moment and reveal how far I am from my real revolution.

I. I Now Understand Myself To Be A Rebel

- I am a rebel. I choose to take my own path untraveled by my friends and family and seek guidance from kind strangers who have wandered down that road before me. I see no other option but ditching the familiar for the unknown. Taking a new approach requires I lockout that critical inner noise and step into adventures that further my confusion and uncertainty.

- I will persist until I succeed. I shall endeavor to walk the path chosen for as long as it takes, with little regard for its endpoint. I will endure because I do not know whether I shall succeed on my first try or my ten thousandth attempt. No fool, I may be forced to change strategies, tactics, plans, jobs, businesses, and even careers, but so long as my hands, heart, and head are aligned with my spirit, I will persist until I succeed.

- I will learn to concentrate on my primary task. I shall not jump wildly from one project to another because that is what undisciplined children do. I will specialize so that my cause and my name are inevitably linked so that when the public says one, they will respond with the other. By focusing on a few good things, I shall gain skills and expertise that will make me a valuable player in the field of battle.

- I will assume the peace negotiator's role in the war between my head's reasoning and my heart's emotions. I will forgo the fears of making grave mistakes in favor of dreaming of all that I will gain. I will not allow myself to be trapped between deciding on the easy route of an austere existence or the bolder course of something grander than what I can comprehend at the present moment.

- Doing nothing is not an option. I receive minimal benefit from choosing to opt-out of decision-making. I can no longer rely on elites' generosity to do my thinking for me, so I must learn how to become my own central command headquarters. Quitting, as a leader of my cause, means letting down my own code of morals as well as my supporters. I am a rebel.

J. I Accept My Purpose Through Wisdom.

- I am a rebel. I can utilize my passions to illuminate future possibilities to my community, but I must have the flexibility to set my own schedules and arrange the jobs I prefer. This lightness of being can temporarily overpower the fears and frustrations of all around me to disappear into the heavens.

- Rebels enjoy fixing messy problems independently that have few parameters. This makes us a valuable commodity should we agree to help out. If things are not working, I can take it apart, reorganize the problem as I like it, and set up new rules. There are renegade opportunities available to us that others recoil in horror from, so when we construct directions from our mind's eye, we can design our own contests.

- I will plan and plot before I proceed. Flagging positive thoughts by recording them reminds me that these ideas are more important than the negative fears and frustration that parade through my mind. I will actively find problems to solve within my sphere of influence. I will write down my goals, strategies, and to-do lists the night before or in the early morning before I get to work because knowing what to do saves me from the burden of not knowing what to do.

- I will not disregard the crisis of negotiating my energy's severing between the person I want to transform into and the soul others want me to be. I will remain tethered to reality while taking refuge in the sunshine of my imagination.

- I will seek the purpose that awakens me, that subverts all impulses to self-sabotage. Despite my pessimistic nature, I will greet my days with a sunny disposition, and a welcoming smile for cheerfulness shortens hard days, and friendly personalities soften all conflict. I will read, live, and play until I find the reason for being more substantial than my tendency to rebel against myself.

- Without a strong reason for moving forward, I may try to study, plan, and prepare, but forces more robust than me will attempt to overwhelm and squash all grand dreams. It is unwise to ignore my true nature just to fit in. I must rebel. I must fight. I must make a ruckus. My birth happened for a reason, and I will do whatever I love and whatever I love is what I am gifted at.

- Despite feeling uncertain about my choices, I no longer need a guarantee of success. I am a rebel, and from this starting line, I resolve to play unconventional pastimes. I shall ignore my inner critic who beats me up for adding another failure to my list of mistakes because my purpose shakes my world like an earthquake awakens a city.

Challenge 1 - I am sorry, you have little choice but to begin your journey into the darkness to find your light. Or maybe you already know what makes you powerful beyond all your doubts and inadequacies? Do not be frightened by this task, for you may be one little skill or one friendly person away from unlocking your talents and revealing your brilliance.

If you are rebellious in nature, falling in line and doing what you are told is not your playhouse. You were born to disrupt, subvert, and change the narrative. Your presence is requested to discover your personal freedom and liberate others from their fears. Sit with this idea and let it wash over you until you are ready for the next step.

NOTES

CHAPTER 2

Okay, Decide Already!

I must apologize, for I may have led you astray just a bit. There were hints here and there in chapter one, but we must address the elephant in the room. A few paragraphs in one book is probably not going to dislodge this particular program in your head as the grooves and patterns have embedded themselves in your psyche for decades. Still, I must mention this before we proceed.

Do you believe that success trappings like wealth, fame, beauty, and exclusivity will be enough to make you happy till the end of your days? There is some truth to that because, on the whole, rich folks are more satisfied than impoverished communities. However, there are mountains of evidence that concluded success does not equal the kind of happiness you desire at all.

Please do not go chasing waterfalls and butterflies searching for your purpose, for your Shangri-la may exist only in your head.

This notion that you must find your goal as a great leader, hero, business owner, or political activist might not be entirely accurate. Comedian Jim Carrey famously said, "I think everybody should get rich and famous and do everything they ever dreamed of so they can see that it's not the answer." Take that to heart; my analysis says that it's true.

You do not have to become a movie star, NFL receiver, rap god, fashionista, Instagram influencer, NBA guard, oceanographer, or Wall Street trader to become happy! Nor do you need to join a monastery or feed children in Africa. All these stories are pleasant fantasies to distract us from the mundane existence we face because most of us are in the wrong profession or doing work that does not suit us.

I believe much of the world's misery comes from a mismatch between personality types, interests, passions, and what class of job we have chosen to engage in. There are tech workers surrounded by loud co-workers who desire quiet places, while some librarians yearn to play with singing children. Some work at desks and dream of forests and mountains, while others pave roads & repair roofs, wishing they could pound on computer keyboards. Very few know who they were meant to be and wander into lands of ashen skies and foreboding clouds.

I repeat, just because you have rebellious tendencies does not mean you need to seek enlightenment, find your inner child or discover your spirit animal. Do it for fun, but do not turn your life upside down, causing your family to be passengers in your delusions as you seek to find what cannot be discovered.

Your purpose might be as complicated as spending eleven years transforming into a brain surgeon, or it could be as simple as making more hours to be a compassionate caregiver to a challenged child. Your future roles will likely be the latter, an unsung hero performing unremarkable tasks to contribute to beautiful causes (for most of us).

Many fighters will disregard my words, and in rebellion, fling their soul in search of their own El-Dorado, the lost city of gold. But they will spend their best days wandering in sweltering jungles and subject themselves to dangerous snakes, alligators, and tribes that should not be crossed.

Some Harvard University researchers studied groups of people who stated they felt contentment regularly and discovered that it was not money, fame, or success that made them really happy. What made them cheerful was knowing exactly what they wanted and having the feeling they were making progress. This group is not stuck in their head, not concerned about being the best (or being very good at it) initially. They will do what they do for the love of it.

And how did they find exactly what they wanted? By trying things out. Finding out what they liked and did not like. Trying enough things and failing at them until they found what they loved. In other words, making mistakes was the way to their success.

Ingvar Kamprad is one such man who tried and failed at multiple products until he launched a mail-order business that soon became furniture giant IKEA. Not satisfied with making small profits selling fish and matches, Ingvar took money from his father (a reward for good grades) and experimented with selling various products.

You should do whatever you love and whatever you love is what you are gifted at. Author Barbara Sher claims that you already know what you love to do right now. You know it, but something is holding you back. If Ingvar Kamprad created furniture retailer IKEA in the dark of winter from a small town outside of Stockholm, Sweden, what can you do?

Information is abundant on the internet, so I doubt you have no clue what you want to do. If you can wrestle out of a person his secret dreams, they will tell you exactly what they want.

No, you have not really attempted anything meaningful because you feel uncertain about your choices. You want a guarantee of success so that your inner critic does not beat you up for adding another failure to your list of mistakes. Realize it does not matter if no one likes your work. What matters is that you tried.

Here you are, and there is the prize way over in the distance. In between is a valley of shadows and doubts that you must climb down into and emerge on the other side. Be careful, you tell yourself, there might be danger in the valley. Or perhaps the canyon is safe and empty, and all you have to do is cross it? You won't know until you try.

See, what is in your heart and your mind as to what you really want could be two different things. You are going to have to come to peace with your decision. I think you are still asking, "What should I do?" because you are conflicted between what you were meant to do and the external influences that trap you into decisions that appear safer.

Maybe you want the creativity of being an artist and the wealth of a lawyer too? Perhaps you want to be a police officer, and your family is pushing you toward dentistry? Maybe sought to become an actor, and you failed the auditions?

This inner conflict is a terrible situation because we can't climb on two trains simultaneously. You have to choose one or the other or remain at the train station. Mr. Kamprad of IKEA could have been another fisherman, but he decided to select the track of merchandise on a grand scale. Most of us take the path of least resistance - the one others tell us to accept or the one that minimizes chances of failure even though it's the wrong path for us.

In my mind, you have three choices:

1. Do nothing and go nowhere.
2. Do what you think others believe is the best option.
3. Do what you were meant to do.

Did you know it is far worse to make no decision and remain in limbo than make the wrong one? If you choose option two, average choices result in expected low-yield results. The smartest choice, number three, will likely be the hardest because it requires the most risk and most effort.

The noise of the world is overwhelming and hinders us from thinking about what really matters. To make a dramatic change, you might require taking a break from your everyday life. You might need time on a beach, hiking in the woods, or a trip to Europe or Africa to reflect on where your life is going. (But you must return to reality expeditiously or get lost in a whole other way)

If you can't hear what's in your heart for some crazy reason, your mind is full of disempowering thoughts, and you will have a long spiritual journey before you. Take tiny chances. Read magazines you never picked up before. Try exotic restaurants that are off the path. Take a community class in something different. Get away from your routines and experience a brighter life!

At some point, learning and watching are not enough. You have to go and talk to people in that field of expertise you are interested in. Within months you will naturally gravitate towards what you love and drop activities that feel like a life being blanketed by gray clouds.

As a creative and rebellious writer, I have difficulty following norms and conversions. Basically, I am in my head more than I would like, completely ignoring my senses and surroundings. Rules and structure are absolute musts for me. Fixed working hours, lunch periods, and closing times help me keep going off the rails. Otherwise, I would work sporadically and indulge in time wasting pleasures.

My recommendation to some of my rebellious friends is to seek regulations provided by the military, ministry, corporations, or other large organizations. You need a vast and expansive reason for being that requires all your energy and devotion, and living under some rules gives the structure you need. Your cause has to shut out the noise of your mind that protests your decision making and a partial retreat can set up future wins.

I am sorry that part of your mind wants to be king of the world and master of all that you survey. You can't have everything in the world because everyone wants that too. Should you avoid accidents, war, and disease, you have a maximum of a hundred and ten years or 40,150 days, to achieve everything and experience the billions of options available to you.

Your irrational mind sees you are compensating to be a landscape architect, master electrician, ER nurse, or criminal judge and says, "is that it? That's all you want? There is so much more out there." Your emotional mind rebels against limits placed against it, and your logical mind says, "come on, we have to pick something."

If you have a rebellious personality, working in a coffee shop or washing cars is a violation of the expansive nature inside you to seek freedom, adventure, and opportunity. Do not settle your soul under a lifetime of gray skies.

Of course, I don't know your particular combination of talents, personality, and experiences, so take my advice with a grain of salt. But when it comes to work-life balance, I must put my foot down! If you are forced to work at a Megamart kind of store or on an assembly line, don't let your hours of labor take over your life. Give yourself space to disrupt the universe and paint your name on this thing we call life.

You need more significant causes like protesting deforestation, or feeding stray animals, or running the best boutique restaurant in town. Then you can start to ignore the rules, violate conventions, and stick it to the man. (Old hippies know what I am talking about).

It is unwise to ignore your true nature just to fit in. Rebel. Fight. Make a ruckus. You were put on this earth for a reason, and part of that reason is to help make some changes around here.

Challenge 2 - I don't think too highly of malcontents who go through life-consuming and complaining about machinations that our ancestors could not dream of. Their lack of gratitude towards the benefits of technology, democracy, law & order, and capitalism is astonishing. It also reveals a deep level of ignorance and awareness how tough life used to be.

Can you be grateful for what you have and for those around you? Even if your car, friends, family, and job are of low quality, be grateful that they exist. If you make a list of ten items you are thankful for, you will feel better.

NOTES

CHAPTER 3

Learn How to Dream As a Rebel

Someone very wise once said that we fear changing ourselves because it's simple to picture what we will lose from our failure to transform, while it is challenging to imagine what we acquire when we achieve our goals.

Isn't it obvious? You can remember the faces of your current friends, family, and co-workers by looking through your phone. Can you visualize what kind of friends and work situation you will acquire in the future? I cannot, and I believe only the clairvoyant can read the stars for the future after sundown.

With this challenge in mind, success requires breaking familiar things and replacing them with what you really need. You must change to see change. Necessary skills are lacking at this present moment to get to where you want to go. If you already had the essential abilities, you would be proceeding to desired destinations.

Not that you are not wonderful already - you are. Please accept the reality that you can't recognize new worlds of possibilities without learning new talents.

When you are inclined to accept further evolution, the next question becomes; how do you become a more dependable and skilled person who is going places? Go ahead and do what you want, when you want. You are intelligent enough to appreciate that learning does not stop the minute you get your diploma. Growth is a lifelong commitment for the victorious.

People expect insignificant things from characters like us. Why do you resist understanding what you are capable of? Your brave heart is shielded from critical eyes, and you have the potential to do remarkable actions for those you care about (that is, if you could get your act together).

People are observing, and the envious can't comprehend the magnificent thoughts and wondrous plans in your head. The public can only witness the results of your actions. Our actions in private practice, unobserved and unmarked, define us more than how we act in public. We are better than that!

Dreamers Shun Critics & Run Over Barriers

I believe we need to go back to the basics. Learn new skills, do the essential work first, and reap the rewards later. Only then can you show your enemies what you are really made of.

Making that change is no longer a should. It's a must because hiding in the backfield of the game and on the sidelines of life no longer satisfies. The sun is going down on your life, and midnight is approaching. Few of us have the future we desire to acquire all that we want.

The shy do not aspire to attempt what you can accomplish because low expectations hold them back. Other personality types feel like they must follow the rules, obey parents, and police what they say, limiting their options. That is not you. Your rebellious nature allows you to break free of these norms and be almost anything you want to be.

Dr. Martin Luther King Jr., the spiritual leader of the civil rights movement, knew he had to break unjust laws to protest African-American segregation from the white population. Speech by speech, King accumulated countless unsatisfied supporters searching for someone who put their darkest fears and brightest hopes into words. A modest and quiet man, King paid the ultimate price for his beliefs.

Many long lonely nights were spent alone with his thoughts. Just like leaders before him, Martin feared the responsibility of leading protesters into dangerous situations where they could be beaten and jailed.

Only after he accepted his transformation from simple preacher to spokesman could he lead nonviolent civil rights protests in the fifties and sixties. King and his followers spent more than a decade in a futile demonstration before winning the Nobel Peace Prize and seeing the Civil Rights Act passed into law in 1964.

Very few of us need to make such sacrifices to make a difference in this world. We just need to find the courage to express our ideas and enroll friends in our projects to help who we can

Find Allies Who Share Your Dreams

Another tragedy of life is that most people talk of their dreams but fail to launch. They project their aspirations in a way that hides their stagnation from their admirers. A minority have capabilities & talents but fear to share these plans, take action, or expand their horizons.

In this divide, the talkers and the doers disappoint in helping one another. Why not break this cycle of failure? Would you consider discussing your desired transformation with those who earn your trust and assemble an action plan to put it into place?

Four Steps To Gaining Clarity As A Rebel. Take what you like and disregard the rest.

Step 1 - Most people are wandering around with this manufactured shell personality, and they are waiting to find friends willing to show their humanity first before they exhibit their true colors. I am just as guilty of this as everyone else. It's our upbringing, you see.

You and I have the uncommon gift of being yourself. Can you reveal some of your vulnerabilities and shine a light on your challenges? Discuss your journey to be the star you believe you can be. No whining, please. All in your secret circle will assist you in mysterious ways to liberate pent-up energy suppressed under your old personality.

Step 2 - What would happen if we began to embrace change rather than resist it? How about tackling the distasteful, dull jobs we all like to postpone until later? What if you put in full effort into all the jobs and tasks that mattered? When you keep your commitments by doing those hard things, each action is like a twinkling star in the night sky. The first few are difficult to see, but as good deeds accumulate, you'll gaze in wonderment at a full constellation of all you have done.

Step 3 - After the sun goes down, the sky darkens to black, and stargazers can just make out the tiny sparkling stars in the moonlight. As though you were an astrologer graphing the night sky, make a note of all your inspirational dreams and ideas on a notepad or video recording. Flagging positive memories by recording them reminds your conscious mind that these ideas are more important than the negative fears and frustration you may feel every hour of the day.

Step 4 - Now go out and actively find problems to solve. It sounds mad because we dislike wrestling with issues that make us suffer and worry. You want more craziness? Be the star others wish for and solve a few of the problems of friends who need help.

If you have difficulty fixing predicaments that are not your own, you won't feel dejected because you are emotionally detached from the outcome. Should you succeed, you might gain the confidence, and inner satisfaction lacked and then blast through your own problems. You may also acquire an impressive reputation and be the bright star among new friends.

Challenge 3 - Need I remind you that you have the intelligence and wisdom that many lack to become a fantastic person, a leader, a mentor, and a teacher? I don't care what your talent is or the field of expertise. If you don't seize this moment, it will be wasted.

There are destitute farmers and shanty town dwellers around the world who would be amazed, even angry, that someone like you had this opportunity amid all this prosperity and blew it. Many of them would trade places with you in a heartbeat because they are overwhelmed with all the support and possibilities you fail to see.

Forgive yourself for working on the wrong things and list all your strengths. What skills are you missing to reach your goals? Forgive yourself for not learning those missing skills in the past. Today is a new day. Can we get a move on, please?

NOTES

CHAPTER 4

Anger Is a Signal, Not a Destination

Self-help books written around positive thinking tend to make me feel happy and then it turns to anger. The idea that you should eliminate all negative thoughts through meditation and affirmations, which are honestly very helpful, is laughable. Gary John Bishop reminded me that many great people launched projects, businesses, and careers from the red hot flames of outrage.

Even the successful fall into despondency or depression, and positive thinking might be the antidote to get them back on their feet. For the rest of us, indulging in blissful thinking without a plan of action is just another senseless pleasure that distracts us from our reason for being. Rebels can benefit from self-help books - let the ignorant jeer - but our biases revolt against simplistic cheerleading & the paint by numbers enthusiasm of "success is easy" authors.

Desiring to eliminate negative emotions is unrealistic and unwise because the more notable your dreams, the more conflict inevitably falls like hailstones as competitors challenge you for resources. You shall inescapably experience severe irritation if you are passionate about your cause. So don't try to eliminate your temper. Instead, manage it.

Anger is a necessary emotion, a psychological response to being offended or hurt that one of our expectations have been violated by someone or something. Why not turn it into an asset instead of a liability by using it correctly?

Angry feelings can guide us in many ways:

- Anger helps us fight for survival.
- Anger assures us when it's time to change.
- Anger warns us to stay away from danger when someone is under pressure.
- Anger helps end the grieving process when dealing with loss,
- Anger fuels and sustains the desire for change.

Where does anger come from? When you lose something, you could feel sadness, disappointment, and anger - it depends on how your mind's blueprint copes with loss. There is a lot of evidence that people who frequently express anger come from dysfunctional homes where members cannot healthily express their thoughts. We can also guess that specific triggers cause angry outbursts, so smart people learn to avoid them.

Clever Rebels Use Outrage Wisely

Whatever the reason, angry souls get frustrated easily and can't handle failure and disappointment like those cool cats we aspire to be. The outraged have a belief system learned, perhaps programmed into their heads, that they should not wait nor suffer unexpected losses.

Which brings us to another form of anger that is rarely expressed - the passive simmering unexpressed anger that the only person feeling it knows about. Millions are walking around full of anger that they keep bottled up inside. This is a gift if you use it correctly.

Rebels are angry because other people hurt them and their internal beliefs told them that they will be punished if they express that anger. They are frustrated that they are working hard and no closer to their dreams than before. They are angry because they are stuck, can't ask for help, and can't be themselves. Does this sound like you?

May I suggest taking your intense rage and dialing it down to feelings of strong irritation? When physically attacked, experiencing death, or when houses burn down, red hot anger is appropriate. For ninety-nine point nine percent of your experiences? No, it is not.

Yet when we get angry over frequent criticism, lousy service, or extra long waits, our rage consumes most of our energy, and we misplace our power for greatness. People lose their patience and grow angry about small things: being overcharged, receiving poor service, and insults from strangers. Mark Manson wrote a whole book about not giving an F...

Please don't waste your time thinking about such trivial things because it costs you more than you realize.

Anger & Contentment Don't Mix

Violent rage is like raining down hailstones on your target, causing colossal damage to your reputation, friendships, and your projects. Challenging opponents require using words filled with negativity, so would you consider turning that hail into the softest rain possible?

Temper your words carefully when you criticize others. Your opponents' goals & dreams may get dampened with your comments, but you have the power to let up and radiate positivity and sunniness.

Napoleon Bonaparte, Emperor of France, was frequently angry and embarrassed about his humble beginnings at the aristocracy's bottom. Thin-skinned, he would fly into fits of rage when others would criticize him. Nevertheless, Napoleon invaded, conquered, and lost continental Europe during the Napoleonic Wars and oversaw society and the law changes. In post-revolution France, his legal code set the first real laws for property, families, and individual rights.

A brilliant military strategist, Napoleon took groups of disorganized French soldiers and turned them into the best marching army of nineteenth-century Europe. Bonaparte suppressed his anger during battles and used his charisma to lead, his intelligence to plan actions, and his fantastic work ethic to manage the details.

Napoleon dominated continental Europe through a series of military victories until he lost most of his army in the Russian winter of 1812. His failings to keep his anger, jealousy, and ego in check cost him allies, and France was finally defeated by British & Prussian (now Germany) forces in the Battle of Waterloo.

One cause of anger is thoughts of jealousy towards others. If you have some ambition to improve your life, you might feel envious when others succeed as you fail. Napoleon was prone to fits of jealous rage, and this behavior helped him work tirelessly to ascend the heights of power. It is also one of the many causes that led to his downfall.

The good news is high performers have used these negative emotions to drive them until they became superior to the people they were envious of in the first place. It also reveals envy is a sign of insecurity, and this feeling you are not good enough won't magically disappear when you are the top dog.

Is it possible that others' jealousy towards you is a mirror reflection of the resentment that you feel towards people doing better than you? Can you be the instigator and victim of envy at the same time?

Now is time to break the cycle of ill feelings. Not that people won't be envious of you if you stop feeling jealous of others - they still will be - it's just that their criticism won't slow you down when you are an unstoppable force of nature.

Our inauthentic world causes an exponential growth of suspicion because we keep our feelings and real personality locked inside. When people who appear to be perfect have good fortune thrust at them, we moan about the unfairness of it all. Most people project their best features, outwards, and conceal their worst flaws. We see them as we think they are rather than who they really are.

Is it not a hilarious farce to discover that we are jealous of people higher up on the food chain, who are envious of those even higher than them? Okay, it is not that amusing because I am implying that no matter how far up the status ladder you climb, you probably will continue to harbor ill feelings for higher society.

Have you seen the humorous picture showing five different fish of various sizes all lining up to eat the next smallest fish? Humans are like that, except we tear each other apart emotionally instead of devouring one another.

Indignation Reminds Us Of Higher Standards

I think that anger is a locking mechanism that keeps us out of the present moment and into our heads, to remember something is not right. Situations that cause anger reminds us how far we are away from our true identity, and it's like being temporarily awakened from our usual zombie-like state.

Use this passionate fit correctly when people try to control or handle you by going in the direction you think is best. If you don't hold your anger, the irritation could also cause you to replay those memories that hurt you on autoplay.

Mental agony sucks your energy out of the present; you fall into the past as you think about this violation. As your anger builds, you reemerge in the present. If unwise, this newly acquired explosion of energy will be directed towards raining down hail on your universe rather than taking actions that cause abundance & prosperity.

Your natural state is to be in a condition of love. You would relish what you do if you followed your real intuition rather than listening to the critical voice in your mind. Your anger arises because you are replaying past pains, keeping you out of the state of love.

It's like observing yourself get unsettled at something that you know is not relevant while your heart grasps you are off the right path. This internal pressure of having your soul split into two grows until external forces ignite the anger.

Rebels don't like warnings, advice, and stupid ideas, and such interference can make us upset. Very few know what makes rebels tick, and what average acquaintances deem is relevant to them doesn't apply to our situation.

Instead, we should watch people who are successful at things we want and take those envious thoughts to induce mild feelings of outrage. A little anger can go a long way to put us into (e)motion and point us in the right direction.

Challenge 4 - Learn to be grateful for your anger. It means you have standards and rules that are not being met. Instead of expressing your anger to people you care about, write down in a journal situations that angers you. Use your anger as fuel to make changes so that you have the life you want.

NOTES

CHAPTER 5

Hatred Will Poison Your Joy

Some people have been burned so badly by life, most of what was good and kind are gone, and nothing but hatred remains. They are in so much pain, their only response is to thunderblast in anger. Hopefully, you do not have a parent, partner, or relative in this state of mind.

It's so easy to blame others for your troubles. Practically everyone does it to the ones closest to them. You would think it's the appropriate response to being hurt, but it is not!

Can you feel the anger inside? Is there someone in your life you hate? At this point, you might feel the hatred flowing through your body. Hate is a natural emotion that is part of who you are. Don't deny its existence, yet don't let it overpower you either.

I believe part of you does not want to become successful because you fear that others will hate you, and you'll respond in hatred at those former friends. But is this fear justified and really worth orchestrating the self-sabotage that you might be doing to yourself?

You might feel a sick pleasure from your hate because you might feel a power within you, an aliveness, that happier folks don't have. Unfortunately, thoughts of harming those who hurt you often trigger feelings of regret, shame, and remorse.

Some people think that anger and hatred fill their body with energy that makes them stronger. All it does is awaken them like a thunderclap to the potential of their strengths. The hate inside can possibly force them to act to achieve a form of revenge, but it does not allow them to enjoy today's pleasure and fulfillment.

Hate is the evil twin of love because it served to damage relationships and separate people from others. Indifference and boredom is the opposite of love and hate since it means you don't care at all. Hatred means you care too much.

Hatred Gives Away Your Power

Targeted hate exists because of emotional attachment. It often occurs because you lost something you loved. Notice that you had a passion that partially defined who you are. If you did not care about the loss, you would feel indifference rather than hate. Hate also implies scarcity because if we can replace the equal value for what you lost, we would cease to hate those who cause it.

Hatred gives the target of your anger all of your power. It does not weaken your enemies unless they respond with their own anger. Then you both lose. If you lost your mind and you slapped someone in the face, both your hand and your enemies' cheek would sting and burn. You can't hurt someone without hurting yourself too.

Some people have gained material success because they were motivated by hate. Some people put them down or beat them up, and these angry people decided to get revenge by accumulating wealth. Good for them. But I question whether they have gained spiritual and emotional success if they live in a hate mindset.

Leonardo da Vinci of Florence, Italy, is claimed to be one of the smartest men to have ever lived. I have to believe he took no notice of the hatred and jealousy of his contemporaries. Da Vinci gave us art, helped us understand human anatomy, and foresaw the age of flight four hundred years before the first airplane. He saw thunderbolts in the sky and predicted the harnessing of electricity.

Leonardo was surrounded by wealthy sponsors and other artisans, and no doubt, he drew inspiration from a wide variety of arts, science, religion, and merchants. Insatiably curious about his surroundings, Da Vinci painted the Mona Lisa and The Last Supper and created sketches of machines that look like bicycles and helicopters centuries before the Wright Brothers took flight across the ocean. What could you create or invest in if you were motivated by inspiration rather than rage?

Why Would You Want To Become A Hateful Radical?

Most people do not benefit from anger. Whether they hate one person or a group of people, their hate brings past memories of hurt and regret; they can't drop their compulsive thinking to concentrate on the present moment.

Hating people absolves you of the responsibilities of running your own life. If someone else is the cause of your pain, then logically, they must also have the solution to end it. Not true. The ending of hatred can only come from understanding how to let go.

We all have unfulfilled wants, like love, security, property, fun, and stability. When we find it or almost get it and then our goal is taken away, it hurts really badly. Our conscious mind searches for the cause because we need to know why and then rain thunder at the person or thing we believe is the cause. So the hatred is the emotional translation of thought, causing pain.

It is in the hater's personal power to choose to eliminate hatred. No one but you controls your own mind, and only you can decide how to respond to your feelings. Hate and anger is the non-acceptance of what happened, of what is. It's natural to feel anger and hostility from time to time and not suppress it, but we should let it go as soon as possible. Living in rage and resisting the truth closes us off to future possibilities.

But how can you replace a murdered child or a parent lost in war or a treasured lost friendship? Loved ones are irreplaceable, but if the people you miss could come back in their proper form of love, they would ask and beg for you to drop the anger and hate in remembrance of the beautiful relationship you once had.

I am no psychologist, but you can turn your hatred into a force for good if you are rebellious in nature. Take all that hatred, all that anger and focus it on something that is causing people pain.

What was said about anger applies to hatred - if you allow many different things to cause you upset, you fuel that anger until you become an angry person. If you hate far too many people, you could transform into a hateful person who seeks to destroy rather than build the world you favor.

Why would you do this to yourself? Learn to forgive yourself and then forgive others. Most insensitive and awful people are stumbling around in the dark themselves, and you happened to get in the way. It takes practice and more patience, but you can train yourself to love so much, you will forget to hate those who dislike you.

On the other hand, you don't want to utterly zen out into a passion-challenged monk who feels little anger or hatred towards anything. There is a danger you might not get enough of those emotional charges to keep moving forward.

What you want to do is take that anger and hate from an out of control boil to a steady simmer so you can become a thunderbolt of power when you need it. Some call it righteous anger. I call it having moral indignation of what is wrong with the world.

Challenge 5 - Would you consider taking this background noise of hate and anger and focusing it on some cause or purpose that gets you riled up? What keeps you up at night because you know it's wrong?

You have the power inside you to fight against so many hateful things. Just pick a cause and go with it. There are so many consumers being exploited, manipulated, and deceived. Children being abused, neglected, and ruined while women are used up, ignored, and underpaid. Voters mislead, angered, and confused. Minorities are beaten, attacked, and jailed every day. If you are a caring and compassionate person, you will never run out of things to get upset about. Pick something.

It is in your nature to fight against injustice, evil, and mistreatment. Be as loud as thunder in a storm and say something. Far too many people are afraid to speak against authority because they are chained by conformity thinking, traditions, and deference to customs that benefit a few while hurting the majority. Unrestrained by such conventions, you can take that which makes you angry and say something meaningful. Will you?

NOTES

CHAPTER 6

Passion Is a Rebel's Salvation

As we are our worst enemy, we exist in day to day lives of stagnation and struggle. How can we become passionate and excited when we keep self-destructing our own plan? That is the cruel dilemma of the rebel tendency.

What a different world it would be if people would flood their lives with more excitement and intensity? Humans are misled that love can only be attained in a lover's embrace. That is only one of many places you can find passion. We can also capture great satisfaction and happiness from our career, calling, children, church, and community.

Ismail al-Jazari of Turkey was another genius who inspired Leonardo da Vinci himself. His book of mechanics, 'A Compendium on the Theory and Useful Practice of the Mechanical Arts,' was enlightening in technology and engineering while Europe suffered during the dark ages.

Al-Jazari instructs us on the design, manufacture, and assembly of machines he invented. The instructions are so clear that engineers in this century have no difficulty recreating them. Such attention to detail that endured a thousand years requires enormous amounts of sustained passion and enthusiasm. Products that Ismail inspired include the alarm clock, hand-washing devices, and humanoid robots.

When we talk to people who are just going through the motions and then come alive with animation, when the topic becomes exciting and fun, we see a flood of passion. The feeling of being really active, fully awake, and charged up is incredible to behold. Why can't we all be this way?

Passion Will Light Up Your Life

Passion happens when you engage in what you love to do, not when others urge you to do it. Excitement infrequently transpires in the classroom, offices, and factory floor because our managers have boxed us into tasks, titles, and predictable behaviors.

Rebels can utilize their passions to illuminate their community provided they have the flexibility to set their own schedules and arrange the jobs they prefer. This lightness of being can force colleagues' fears and frustrations to take a break for a while.

Passion and excitement are doppelgängers, similar, but different. Love is the friend we are happy to spend time with, while excitement makes the party louder and more joyful. Play with one, and the other may show up.

Many falsely believe that passion and excitement only exist after work with friends and family. Work is a necessary, unpleasant evil of life, right?

I want you to question that belief.

Not all endeavors are backbreaking and laborious. Many wealthy people and artists find enthusiasm in their work. They would instead work than play because they are in a flow state of passion and excitement, living in the present moment.

It becomes harder to work in dreadful jobs and also be passionate in our playtime. We are not on and off switches. We are people. When we are unhappy with our home lives, this feeling will flow over to work life, and if we are unhappy at work, it will flood over into the rest of our lives.

It is easy for me to see why so many people work unhappily in jobs they would preferably not do. Not only are their jobs routine and boring, but they also do not have to control their pay or their schedule.

Workers don't know whether their work is meaningful or if it actually benefits the world at large. Even if employees perform highly skilled and valuable work, schedules become a flood of projects that include dozens or thousands of contributors, so they don't feel ownership over their addition.

Passion Is Work

Once a rebel personality can get their freelance firm or small business into profit, that industry can be a great source of passion and excitement. All the clues of what not to do are revealed in large corporations who take most of their workers for granted and focus on the bottom line profits rather than the community's well being.

The solution for most rebels is to take work that is boring and ordinary and make it fun, challenging, and extraordinary. When their customers can feel how enthusiastic the owner and staff are about their work, they want to come back for more.

Some companies throw parties for customers and/or staff. Others run contests for sales and donation drives. Quite a few use creative ideas to keep product lines fresh and attractive. Work does not have to be emotionally draining and difficult if managers can drown out negativity with a philosophy of fun, passion, and excitement.

Challenge 6 - If you work in a corporate or government environment that dulls your senses and kills your spirit, all you might need is a spark of hope to reignite the passion in your love life and excitement in your hobbies.

Start planning your escape by spending a few hours a week dreaming up your solopreneur idea. Keep working in your day job while using your creative talents to plan out a business or charity you personally find exciting.

Maybe you might change jobs, have another child, or experience some other life event that renders your dream business unnecessary? It does not necessarily matter whether your business or cause takes off or not. What you need is some dream that fires up your passionate soul so you can know what it is to feel truly alive.

NOTES

CHAPTER 7

Diminishing Worrisome Thoughts Untethers Rebellious Souls

This not an easy life being someone who fights against traditions and standards. It may not be an option to fit in, conformity is a more comfortable choice, but our spirit vehemently protests living a life that is a poor fit. While some of us love being rebels without a cause, most fighters are reluctant to do so.

The splitting of our energy between the person we want to transform into and the soul others want us to be is not a clean-cut; we are tethered to reality while taking refuge in the sunlight of our creations. We worry because we know our actions have consequences, and we feel anxious because we would preferably please our community than unavoidably hurt those around us.

Worry is a terrible problem for success seekers because as we try to achieve our dreams, our subconscious mind will create all these nightmare scenarios to stop us from being who we were meant to be. The apprehension will never stop until we abandon our goals or overcome our fears through sheer persistence.

It's nothing more than a mental habit that feels like we are getting something done as we wait for life to reveal its shining rewards. As a child, you watched your parents worry and now emulate them because that is how mothers and fathers behave. Maybe you concluded that worrying is a way of staying in control because you can prepare for future problems before they happen.

Worrying Is A Hard Way To Love

Is it possible that hearing "I was worried about you" felt similar to bathing in the warm rays of sunshine, glories of concern and appreciation? Could you possibly think that worry equals love? Maybe the act of reverence has little to do with the person receiving the attention and more to do with the worrier's emotions of insecurity? Talk about getting mixed messages.

How can you not worry as well if you are trying to please too many people at the same time? Each person has conflicting demands, and we can't move forward without disappointing someone we care about. Instead of taking one side or another in a contest, we often do nothing and keep our minds busy imagining their reactions when they discover our ineptitude.

You know why we keep behaving this way? If we believe that worrying helps us, we will seize evidence that our worries come true to justify our behavior. If we search hard enough, we can point to situations where we are worried, and reality confirmed our suspicions. "See, I was right. My worries are justified." We create our own propaganda because we shun the awful truth that we may be acting irrationally.

Are you worried about so many things that most of what you stew about does not come true? Most of our apprehensions never become a certainty, and we waste time living under dark clouds of anxiety instead of the bright sunshine of optimism because of it.

If you knew that ninety to ninety-five percent of your fears will never come true, would that make you less anxious?

For some, life is so tough, almost every waking moment is spent in worry until the danger passes. Imagine having to escape slavery just to have a chance to bask in the sunshine of freedom? Frederick Douglass was born into slavery on a plantation in Talbot County, Maryland, in 1818. In September 1838, Fredrick disguised himself as a sailor, escaped to New York, and modified his name from Bailey to Douglass to avoid detection.

Do your worries pale in comparison? If caught, Frederick would have been put back into chains and shipped to another southern plantation. Douglass gained an education to become a well-known orator and abolitionist and went around the country, speaking out about the evils of slavery. He even advocated for President Lincoln's cause and helped African-Americans to enlist in the American Civil War.

When we tell ourselves not to worry through will power, we will fail within minutes because we ask our conscious minds not to do something our subconscious mind wants to do. That is like telling a thief to guard the treasure.

Worry is really a lack of confidence in ourselves to handle new challenges. On one side, individualists want to revolt against the norm by doing new things others rarely do. On the other side, we feel anxious about joining those revolutionary game-changers who break the rules and move society to innovative solutions.

Many of us try to avoid changes; the unknown can feel like a permanent nighttime to our everyday & cloudy existence. We are silly that way. Our subconscious is trying to protect us by avoiding potentially dangerous actions, and anxious feelings can't see past the fog of our imagination.

Shatter Endless Rumination By Staying Active & On Purpose

The more time we live in the present, embracing our natural rebelliousness without overthinking it, the more chances we will have to challenge these assumptions. My favorite Shawshank film quote is "Get busy living, or get busy dying." Worrying is dying ten thousand deaths in your mind, taking action is a daily rebirth. Your choice!

Sharing our worries with others or displaying signs that we have anxious thoughts makes the community's collective anxiety worse. Just like laughing and smiling can be contagious, so can unpleasant nervousness and sadness. I read that if a friend of a friend expands her tummy from overeating, you might add a few pounds yourself as you contract a craving for midnight snacking too. I hope this theory is disproved as false!

Maybe your whole family is a bunch of worrywarts, and being around them causes you additional stress? No, you can't run away from your children or make your mother-in-law walk the gangplank. Can you construct a life where you live with negative people but don't participate in their whining & complaining?

Bottling up your feelings is no solution either. Keeping your thoughts to yourself may result in tight shoulders, stiff movements, frowning, and griping until you explode in rage or collapse in depression. No, you have got to express your sentiments to someone. Can you elect excellent listeners or mentors who have the know-how to reframe negative perceptions into incredible possibilities?

Challenge 7 - Forgiveness is the best key to overcoming worrying. If you had great parents, they quickly forgave you for your mistakes because your happiness was of a higher purpose than what the neighbors might think. As an adult, you must parent yourself to build your resiliency so you can get up quickly whenever someone knocks you down to the ground.

You forgave others because it gives you a sense of inner peace, and you forgive yourself because you want to be free of thoughts that remind you how pathetic you can be. With a clean slate, you can renew old friendships and have a fresh attitude towards starting new ones.

Our minds will not accept that worry is very bad for us until we give it massive evidence that those thoughts are false. Observe non-worriers, handle what you fear, and then go out and do it yourself. When you are kinder to yourself, you realize that you can take on anything.

NOTES

CHAPTER 8

In A Desert Of Lies, Trust
Your Intuition

If you are struggling, I swear with certainty, you are trying to look into the future to see what is on the horizon, which is like watching the approach of a sandstorm formed into mysterious, fiery clouds.

None of us can see into the future, the unknown, and so we have to guess the best we can with our intuition. The gut feeling in your stomach and chest alerts you whether it is safe to proceed or unwise to move forward.

I question whether you really trust your intuition on difficult decisions. If you are an excessive worrier or frequently procrastinate on things that others find trifling, you don't know how to listen to your gut feeling. You gotta cut that out and start paying attention.

Marie Forleo, coach & podcaster, says if your intuition feels tight or constraining, then it's a big fat NO! However, if your gut feeling is expansive and excited, then proceed with caution. It's a GO!

Choosing not to listen to your intuition can put you down some wrong roads. Some of us respond by postponing decisions until outer forces us to, some let others make decisions for them, while most copy whatever the majority does, right or wrong.

You are not like everyone else, and much of the knowledge at your feet does not apply, so do not follow the crowd. Your fears will steer you astray, and you may have to pay a hefty penalty for your lack of faith.

Little to do with your level of intelligence - your IQ score has nothing to do with the effectiveness of your decision-making ability. What I mean to say is, if you experience continuous rejection, have failed on many accounts, or your parents have restricted your options, you are probably making decisions automatically that have the least amount of risk and thinking.

Decisions Are Difficult Because You Lack Systems & Principles

Let me tell you a story of six blind villagers. One day, they heard an elephant traveling nearby. Since none of the men had seen this type of animal before, they were curious to examine it. The men gathered around the elephant, and each reached out to touch it with his hands.

The first blind man felt the elephant's trunk and told his companions, "this feels like a big snake. Elephants must belong to the snake family of animals. The second blind man touched the foot of the elephant and said, "no, you are wrong. She feels like a tree, so it must have the shape of a tree." The third blind man put his hands on the elephant tusks. "Ah, I feel a spear. Elephants are built like a spear.

"You are all wrong. Elephants are more like a stone wall," said the fourth blind man as he ran his hands along the side and belly of the elephant. "No, no, no," said the fifth blind man who had his fingers on the tail. "Elephants are exactly like ropes. I am sure of it", The sixth blind man screeched out, "What are you saying? Elephants are like giant palm leafs" He was touching the big ears of the creature.

And so each blind man yelled at each other, until the quarrel was broken up, convinced that he was right and that everyone else was wrong.

Some people would say this story does not apply to them because they have the gift of sight. True. But just like Arab caravans amid a sandstorm, they can't see other people's point of view. Their rigid viewpoints and ideas are like the sand blinding their eyes. Neither do they ask those standing in different places, nor do they move closer to their opponents to experience what they feel.

Had each of the six blind men walked around the elephant or discussed plainly what they touched, all six would have benefited from seeing the whole animal, and each would gain higher wisdom. Instead, they argued with each other and only gained a piece of information and not the whole.

The wise and the foolish are not that different from the six blind men. We become fixed in our opinions when wandering in our own deserts of possibility. Even rebels stop learning and only retain pieces of knowledge that are not enough to move forward. Do you think we can make the right decisions if we only have part of the data required?

Compounding our failing decision making is a lack of concentration. Our attention spans decrease due to social media, television & work, and we keep looking for the next best thing.

Businesses know consumers succumb to boredom quickly, so they develop new products that are more useful than previous offerings. We are conditioned to throw out the original and purchase newer versions. After all, everyone else is doing it. This hurts society more than you realize.

Real-life is often dull as sand. Most can't take the silence of their surroundings. Doing nothing is intolerable. When it's quiet, we hear our negative thoughts, and we drown the silence with music, TV, or talking.

Your mind is equipped to look for excitement and entertainment to relieve boredom and anxiety. Your mind hates to focus, but possessing concentration is the best way to build skills that create wealth and value in the world.

We have as many choices as grains of sand in the Sahara desert that our head spins. Every generation wants to experience as many stories, films, shows, music, and dishes as they can. With such possibilities, many of us skip from one thing to the next...

Adding to this sandstorm of misinformation, insufficient data, and unlimited choices are the opinions of others, most of which are reckless impositions on our consciousness. Our minds are clouded with conflicting rules of conduct imposed by people who desire quick and easy solutions that make things worse and not better.

For example, when Milton Hershey was just starting out, he experienced numerous failed endeavors. First, he worked as a printer's apprentice and was fired. Then Milton went into business, only to disappoint in two more ventures. By the time he was twenty-six years old, he was penniless.

If you think Mr. Hershey was falling from a deficit in character, you have not been paying attention. My guess is he suffered from the same flawed decision-making process as everyone else, that is until he discovered his real purpose in life. Hershey found his calling in the candy-making business.

I know it's hard to make decisions that matter. Have you ever tried to get five people to decide where to go to eat? It takes endless debates about the merits and benefits of each location until all possibilities are exhausted. The unofficial leaders influence their dining companions to make final decisions when the moment arrives. We, rebels, are a pain in the ass because whatever the group decides, we tend to disagree with the consensus.

We must develop the strength to choose what is best for us. We are torn apart inside by conflicting desires. Maybe our investors or parents want us to do something, but our inner voices tell us to do the opposite.

Once Mr. Hershey established a caramel candy factory, it would have been safer to continue making candy. Despite protestations from his backers, more massive dreams drove him to expand his business. What he really wanted to make was milk chocolate that was affordable to everybody. And he did, as every American who devours Hershey chocolates can attest to.

Rebels Don't Follow The Rules, We Make The Rules

If you have a rebel personality, you may enjoy fixing messy problems that have few parameters. If things are not working, you can take it apart, reorganize the problem as you like it, and set up new rules. There are renegade opportunities available to you that others chose to ignore. If you can handle working as an individual, following directions of your own making, the world may roll out the red carpet for you.

Specialize in difficult things, and you can't help but win. Other personalities do not like ambiguity the way you do. Most people would instead tackle simple issues or outsource complicated problems to those who can. When you can concentrate on one thing, your thing, you could experiment a little until you find a sequence of decisions that leads consistently to the results you desire.

The quality of your life depends on the quality of the decisions you make. If you are deferring or avoiding making decisions, then someone will make them for you. Do you enjoy giving up your power? Do you like the compensation awarded to you? If you want to gain control over your life, you need to start to make your own decisions.

Challenge 8 - Your decisions should answer the main question, "What do I do next?" in each new situation by narrowing the scope. To do this, you must structure the question to eliminate most of the other possibilities. When you form a query by dropping all other options, you simplify the problems to get more specific and accurate answers to bring you the desired results.

If you are not living the life you want, your decisions are missing this specificity, and your questions are too general and ambiguous for you to get anywhere. I know pushing you into a corner makes you want to run and escape, but if you choose your own corner, you get to build the life you want. A lack of decision making means you could become a laughable wandering desert nomad who has not pitched their tent and staked out a claim.

NOTES

CHAPTER 9

Some Mistakes Are Friendly, Some

When you strive to break free from anything your social circle has done before, you may obtain more innumerable mistakes than anyone you know. Take that to the bank. Many wealthy folks have advised in numerous books, "Should you desire to become rich quickly, make lots of small mistakes as fast as possible, so you stumble on the best alternative before the competition does."

Now, I must rain on your parade and remind you of the caveat to this strategy. Except for the grace period of childhood & teenage rebellion, our liberal culture continues to punish adults who commit more mistakes than they deem acceptable. Can you see the potential conflict between what affluent investors do and working-class rules?

Remember being laughed at when you said something others thought was backward? Recollect failing your school tests and made to feel stupid. Remember missing the team cutoff or not getting that job you wanted? How about bankrupting a business or getting divorced? How many friends and admirers did you lose as they looked elsewhere for leadership and reassurance?

It was not the failure that was as critical as was the reaction from others. Maybe your parents gave you false smiles and said, "you will do better next time?" Perhaps your friends teased and mocked you for being bad at sports, dancing, singing, or whatever your group is into?

 Painful, right? There are societal forces beyond our comprehension that desire to groom you to adapt to a law & order society rigged for the few. The sooner you adjust, the less disapproval you get from others. Oh, it's not all bad. If you know how to game the system, you could potentially reach the penthouse suite yourself.

So you resolved to only take risks where you had a good chance of success. You dropped those activities quickly when you were failing in favor of safer endeavors. It was safer not to take risks and stay within the margins of being average.

This is a big miscalculation we make. Mistakes are like rain in that they feel like a disruptive nuisance to a string of sunny days, but on reflection, errors help you develop the way rain nourishes the grass, trees, and flowers.

The Fear Of Mistakes Is A Form Of Social Control

In some circles, we have been taught to work hard enough to live but not so laborious that friends will give us a tough time trying to make something of ourselves. Other clubs won't tolerate anything but workaholic tendencies, but they also share the same disdain as slackers for free radicals and revolutionary thought. With wisdom and clarity, you must find friends who fully accept you for who you are.

Fidel Castro was in significant peril while successfully leading the communist revolution in Cuba and overthrowing the oppressive dictatorship of Fulgencio Batista. Had he been caught, he would have likely been executed. Your mistakes will cost far less than your life. In fact, for most goals, you are risking very little other than your time and reputation.

You hate losing and making mistakes so much, often you don't even try. You know why? According to experts, we fear loss twice as much as the gains from winning and will spend twice as much effort keeping what we have as trying to get more.

You want more irony? Younger generations want to take the most risks but lack the judgment, experience, and financial backing to make good decisions. Older people have financial assets and a wealth of technical and managerial experiences but are scared to take chances.

A young President Castro of Cuba launched universal health care and improved education in the 1960s, but later as an elder statesman, during the 1980s and '90s, Cuba stagnated under mismanagement and corruption.

Loss aversion keeps you stuck in your job, in a miserable relationship, eating the same awful food, and making the same mistakes over and over again. People make the same faulty logic when they spend half an hour waiting in line at the gas station to save three dollars even though they could have earned fifteen dollars working overtime for thirty minutes. I know you don't do that, right?

If we fear loss twice as much as gain, we will act accordingly. Even if you had a business idea that could make you millions, would you do it if your success could cost you all your friendships? Your mind weights the benefits of future money against the benefits of current relationships and will provide you a logical justification for rejecting the opportunity.

Instead of partnering with Fidel Castro to help turn Cuba from a socialist autocracy into a capitalist democracy, the United States continued its embargo for half a century. The CIA campaigned to assassinate him with over 638 failed attempts. US politicians could not defeat socialism in Cuba because lifting the ban to pursue peace talks could risk political defeat. Sanctions were the safer route. It also meant billions of dollars in lost trade and tourism.

Loss aversion is a symptom of being a compulsive thinker, thinking about the past and future all the time. We can recall the times we lost something precious to us and then resolve to not do anything similar that could be a mistake. When we hide from errors, we inevitably prevent victory because the fastest way to become successful is to make sequential mistakes.

Real thinking is hard. Your mind can't mentally process the pros and cons of decisions with overwhelming stimuli of sounds, lights, colors, and patterns in front of you. Exhausted by it all, we use what seems like instinct but is really the fears, worries, and thoughts of your subconscious. So your determinations are not really decisions - you are doing what was safe in the past. Your past is making your decisions for you.

Some people are far more fearful of taking risks than others. They watch the rain forecast on television and fear catching a cold or slipping on the pavement. Children notice the rain through the soaked window and run around the house looking for their galoshes and raincoats. Which faction do you belong to?

Factual Knowledge Reduces The Fear Of Mistakes

Experienced entrepreneurs have learned how to judge risk naturally, as wealthy people are less risky gamblers than rash amateurs. Stories of millionaires in a casino betting a hundred thousand dollars on one roll of the dice are rare comical errors of judgment.

More urban legend than fact, winning gamblers don't need to go for big jackpots to fight their fear of losing.

The wealthy become rich by taking countless small, low-risk actions that yield more profits than losses. Successful innovators can also ignore doom's voice in their head and make decisions based on facts and figures rather than imagined fears. They also consider their mentors and friends' input rather than running their past thoughts as an excuse not to take action.

I did advise you in the previous chapter to use your intuition as a guide. That is your fail-safe option in the absence of useful data. When you get closer to the top, it becomes easier to purchase the right information necessary for success. In that case, listen to the numbers and accept input from your advisors.

As you accumulate knowledge and wealth, you might just find that your mistakes are as commonplace as failing to pack an umbrella and getting caught in the rain. So you got a little wet? It's no big deal at all.

Challenge 9 - To beat the fear of making mistakes, we must take a leap of faith and reduce our worries about the consequences of losing. Understand the downside, and move forward. We need to follow the examples of others who are successfully taking smart, calculated risks.

As another forgiveness exercise, could you write down a list of five major mistakes you made? Be your own therapist and tell yourself it is okay that you did not succeed in those situations. These learning experiences made you stronger. You need to forgive yourself, so you lose the fear of making future mistakes.

NOTES

CHAPTER 10

Pain Is Inevitable, Suffering Is Not

I don't know what is causing your suffering - divorce, bullies, crime, debt - all I know is that your mind never wants to experience those emotions again and configure you to what is familiar and safe. Suffering exists in a state of mind that lacks knowledge that you can follow rather than the external threat itself. See, if you knew what to do with certainty, you would be doing it right now instead of sitting in pain.

Suffering, like a cascading waterfall of ceaseless thoughts, is part of life. For example, death is something that we can't avoid, so we must endure, like the rock in the stream. We must grieve for a while and then move on.

The key is to push on at some point. You must choose a plan of action, even if it's wrong, or you might let yourself drift to a place where others will take advantage of and manipulate you.

Our subconscious minds are scared of change. Many hate the unknown and will do anything to stop our world from turning. Instead, people would prefer to remain in a known hell where their thoughts fall out of their subconscious in an unending waterfall of tears than risk traveling down the river into a sacred pond of tranquility.

If you are a worrier, your pessimism is waterboarding your optimistic energy because you believe something terrible will happen in the future. Even when our conscious mind knows we are beating ourselves up for no good reason, it can not overpower the subconscious's irrationality.

So this leads to a paradox of choice. If we rebel against something we don't like, we might end up being controlled by something even worse. When we turn down job after job because we don't like it, we could tumble over a dangerous waterfall into unemployment and poverty.

Would you believe that unemployment can be a more deadly form of misery than producing work that does not match our talents and interests? Some tragically die from broken hearts when they have no purpose for being. If we self-sabotage too much from our principles, we could do more than suffer in silence; we can fall into a spiral of depression that is difficult to shake.

To me, depression is a morse feeling of crawling rather than hiking through suffering. Everything feels more formidable, and getting through the day is a higher priority than any mythical dream in the future. Asking a depressed person to seek their purpose or achieve higher powers is insensitive. First, they must accomplish normalcy before resuming any resistance against poverty, wrongdoers and injustice.

Suffering Is A Social Construct Of Human Insensitivity

Can I propose a very radical idea? What if depression, alcoholism, and drug addiction may not be entirely mental diseases created solely by the sufferer's mind but endure significant influence by external forces?

Our rebellious personality makes us feel sick because we must submerge ourselves in a toxic and harmful culture that we are forced to live in. We live in this society, but it is not compatible with our needs and desires. We don't want to trade our lives for scientific-industrial-professional careers with set rules & cultures in return for materialistic pursuits. Our passions lie elsewhere.

We rebel, suffer, and fall into states of depression because our culture is designed to transform you into a conforming consumer forced to swim in the raging rivers of the global economy. It does not care about your needs, values, passions, or goals. You are a labor input meant to go to school, work, produce children, consume, and retire. Some desire such a life and thrive in it, but rebels do not.

You thought there was something wrong with you? Like you were broken? Maybe you are more like a flower or tree growing near the banks of an overflowing river? How could living things not become sick in an unhealthy environment?

If we are bombed with constant stimuli with endless choices of what to see, who to visit, and what to do, our tired minds become stressed. No one teaches us how to manage our minds or how to strategically plan for success. And the ignorant blame us & turn sufferers into pariahs because it must be our fault!

Depression could be the default way of coping with life by shutting down the senses and numbing ourselves from the pain of greed, negativity, and selfishness. (Yes, some mental distress may be wholly caused by biological & genetic factors. The suffering person can also create their own misery through mistakes, bad luck, & poor habits. I acknowledge this theory does not hold for all.)

Why some people can bounce back from illness, death in the family, or layoffs while others fall into misery. Is it possible that people with diseases and addictions like drug abuse, alcoholism, gambling, and depression are hypersensitive to the malicious behavior and message we are all getting? They retreat inside their minds, which are already filled with negative beliefs, making them more likely to replay past memories.

Maybe most people have stronger immunity and can block out all the bad news, crisis, and world problems, but we, the minority, can't. Rebels do not have or never learned a better coping mechanism? I don't know why pain is inevitable. I also believe suffering is not.

Mahatma Mohandas Gandhi suffered much in his pursuit of the liberation of the Indian nation from British rule. Greatly influenced by Henry David Theroux and Tolstoy's works, Gandhi used principles like satyagraha (truth-force), ahimsa (nonviolence), and civil disobedience as tools to fight oppressive regimes. He did not wait for others to rescue his nation, nor did he give up when there was no indication his strategies were working.

Many believe the solution is in the future and not today, so we keep waiting and waiting. We might even endure terrible abuse today, like a child standing under a waterfall, pounded by the force of the water because we presume that the rewards are worth the wait.

The dilemma is the ideal future never arrives. The liquid flow does not cease, and the teacher will not appear to order the child out of the water. Tomorrow becomes today, and the suffering continues.

We run our memory banks searching for the solution, but we can't find it. Yes, we can find programs to make our beds, cook meals, drive a car, but we don't have the experience or plan to deal with what is causing our suffering. Just like our mothers and fathers rescued us as children, we are waiting for someone else to save us.

We think:

1. The problem exists, 2. I have never done it before, 3. It hurts, 4. I am helpless, 5. My parents took care of problems in my youth, 6. The answer is to wait for a substitute for my parents to solve my problems.

Asking for help is not the same as requesting others do the work for us. You are making one of three mistakes. Either you don't know how to handle your problems, or you are not asking for help or asking the wrong people for help. What is the saying? You should look for a hand up and not a handout if you want to get far in life?

End Suffering With Your Hands, Not Your Mind

Suffering ends when you decide to put faith in yourself and not in your past experiences. It's time to drop the idea that the ending of distress is a future event. It's something that happens now, this minute, this second.

As you read this book, you are not aching - you were concentrating on understanding these ideas. Now let your mind drift, and when you are back into your old thoughts, you resume your suffering. That is the clue, action.

Take action. Do something you feel is taking towards your goals, and your grief may lessen. Your thoughts of worry and anxiety may even disappear as you immerse yourself in your work.

You will never overcome your fear of success until you disturb the state of mind that causes your suffering. Your pain won't go away until your thinking changes, and your reasoning won't improve until you take a new radical set of actions. These actions won't be apparent to you until you embrace the unknown within the present moment.

Challenge 10 - People put on brave faces and won't admit they have a problem until they are in a crisis. Millions are afraid of being found out (their secrets) because they could risk their economic and social standing. They are slow to trust new friends and partners because of old emotional baggage.

Can you forgive the people around you for their flaws so you can move on? For example, should your friend lose her temper, snap at you, ignore her missteps, and change the topic. Believing that others' ill will is always an attack on you raises the prospect that you will engage in frequent arguments, which will increase your suffering.

When she sees you are not abandoning the relationship, either she will continue to misbehave, or she may make amends to repair the hurt. You don't have to accept abusive behavior, but it's unwise to quit at the first sign of trouble as well. Blaming others, engaging in conflicts, standing your ground in petty arguments - these are all excellent ways to suffer in silence.

NOTES

CHAPTER 11

Rebels Are Not Their Past,

They Are The Future

Are you not exhausted spending your life trying to figure out what is real and what is not? It could be convincingly argued that every non-fiction book reveals its whole story by breaking through a storm of lies, myths, and falsehoods before revealing a rainbow of truths. Much of what we believe to be true is not so and conflicts ignite all over the internet because there are parties who are beneficiaries of this deception.

Hey, don't shoot the messenger! I am just passing on what it took me years to realize - we are surrounded by lies, deception, and misinformation, and you can only discover your personal truths by moving beyond that which was freely given to you.

And then there is you, my rebellious friend. What is something that others believe in that you do not? I know that a life of conformity, fitting in, and doing whatever is popular is not for us, and we have to revolt against those lies people tell us to find our own way.

Everything you learned as a wee one, you must question as an adult. All your childhood lessons and experiences - you saw it through the fresh eyes of a kid, now you must audit it from the wise vantage point of a mature being.

Now that you have acquired a good reason for why you were stuck all these years let's go back to the beginning...

Children Are Brilliant At Learning But Unwise In Their Interpretation

We are receiving thousands of bits of information every minute, far more than previous generations ever did. Our minds can't cope with all that information at a conscious level; therefore, we see, hear, smell, touch, and taste data processed via our subconscious mind instead of our rational mind.

Your conscious mind is the part you are aware of - it's logical, calculating, and responsive to the outside world. These words you are reading are processed with your conscious mind. Your subconscious mind is where the vast majority of your brain activity is. It regulates your breathing, blood, organs. It stores all the information you need including names, history, people, skills, and everything you need to be a functional being.

Habits like driving, riding a bike, brushing teeth, using phones, and all our values and beliefs are learned in the conscious mind and transferred to the subconscious mind.

That way, you can do things without being consciously aware of all the body movements and thoughts required to do simple things like talk, walk, and react. We do this to function, grow, and develop ourselves into adults who can concentrate on dangers and opportunities, leaving the trivial and routine running on autopilot.

The subconscious is naive because it believes anything if you perform it enough times from a young age. Subconscious brains have to open to new ideas, or we would all remain in a baby-like state of mind. Children don't have filters to judge truth from fiction, at least not in the beginning. You can convince someone to believe in anything that is not true by repeating your argument again and again rather than using logic to persuade them.

Don't you get it? Everything your parents taught you as a child, stupid or intelligent, gets lodged in the back of your mind, in the silent part of your brain. It is not your fault that you believe things people ridicule you for. You had little power in your ability to sensor disempowering beliefs!

Our parents always worried about our safety because, as children, we took pretty reckless chances with our bodies. I know you heard "NO" or "STOP. Don't do that, naughty boy!" Far more than "YES" or "OKAY, go ahead." Let's not blame our parents for our problems. They did a pretty good job keeping you alive, fed, and clean, did they not?

Could you hear the voice of your parents saying "no, don't do that' in your subconscious every time you try something new and scary? Could you be stopping yourself from moving forward because your mind has tens of thousands of memories, all telling your subconscious mind 'stop, danger, be careful'? This causes you to abandon all efforts once you get started?

Teach Yourself To Overwrite Childhood Programming With New Stories

If you thought there was something wrong with you and all it was that your original programming was defective, you could change some of it. If you can overwrite the harmful prescriptions with new habits that install success behaviors, you can change who you are.

Even if you repeat something positive consciously three times a day, your subconscious mind repeats negative ideas acquired during your childhood thousands of times a day. It took you years to become a negative person, and so it will take you months and years, not days, to transform into an upbeat personality.

And this brings us back to today. As an adult, you have chosen an identity, a way of being, and from this maturity, you can look back on your childhood and see your mistakes. While you will always be a student of life, you can also assume a teacher's role—an instructor who can hold themselves accountable for slacking off, for not putting in the work.

Your assigned education plan? Discover your mental and emotional limits by exploring your passions. Dive into the areas of concern that you feel you can make a difference. Sitting on a deck chair on the beach or log cabin hoping for a rainbow to appear is not an option. You must investigate things you have never experienced before to teach yourself better philosophies than those received in infancy.

Only then will you bump against the harsh reality of truth - quite a lot of what you believed in as a child and young adult are false. It was never real, and your thinking was holding you back.

For example, most of us believe having failures and making mistakes can be painful and economically devastating. In truth, all your mistakes have made you the person you are today. Had you not failed from time to time, you would have not learned hard lessons and would have been unable to mature into a functioning adult.

John Paul DeJoria made multiple mistakes before becoming an extremely wealthy man. He spent his past with an LA gang before joining the military. After working for Redken Labs and selling encyclopedia book sets door to door, the salesman created John Paul Mitchell Systems with his partner Paul Mitchell. All his failures built up his character to this point so he could withstand the next major crisis in his life.

John's wife left him at the launch of his shampoo company, and his wealthy investor backed out, leaving him with no support or funding. John gambled on a seven hundred dollar loan and paid the printer & bottler all he had. He started selling the company's shampoo from salon to salon, living out of his car with his son until the business took off.

Can you see that he took all the negative thoughts of his childhood in foster homes and weighed it against the successes he had as an encyclopedia salesman? DeJoria built himself a mental ramp out of poverty and into the business world using rich life experiences and discarding what did not serve him.

Your thoughts are not entirely your own. They are a composite of everything you saw and experienced - television, movies, music, newscasts, internet, gossip, teachers, parents, friends, parties, work, travel, books, festivals - so you have to sort through it all to find the gold inside the dirt. Just like John Paul DeJoria and other entrepreneurs have done before you.

All that negative chatter in your head, calling you stupid, idiot, loser, and failure? Those are the echoes of your childish thoughts that blamed you for failing to meet others' expectations.

The ultimate middle finger to your inner critic is to go out, attempt new things, fall over and over, and come to the realization that it does not matter. It never did.

No one needs to know about your mistakes or the lessons learned from failures. They fade away like the remnants of rainbows when outbursts of sunshine chase away gray clouds. Your tombstone will keep your secrets for you. What matters is how you will be remembered, how you made them feel while you lived.

Challenge 11 - Failure is your friend because it, paradoxically, makes you wiser. You learned a new way of not succeeding. For that, you should express gratitude. How about writing down five failures and thinking of five benefits you gained from these failures?

This may sound crazy, but when you reframe your belief that 'losses hurt you' into a new religion that 'failures make you stronger and wiser,' disempowering opinions no longer have the power to control you. Repeat after me: "I am grateful for my failures because I learn more from them than my successes." If you really believe this concept, you won't feel devastated whenever you fall down. You may even get up and ask for more.

NOTES

CHAPTER 12

Radical Souls Know Wealth &
Popularity Is Not Enough

Let's tackle your overly obsessive thinking. Have you considered that your high level of intelligence makes you question things, and then these compulsive queries cause you to sit in a state of mind that can't enjoy the swirling of unanswered thoughts?

Would you agree that children and adults who avoid compulsive thinking can get more out of life more than you can? I would tell you to stop, but we know I am asking an unreasonable request.

It may dawn on you that you instinctively know what makes you successful or miserable but believe acquiring more fabulous fortunes should necessitate holding out a little longer.

Let's face facts. You procrastinate to eliminate those habits that make you unhappy because you are getting a secret benefit or pay-off. Like married couples who believe passionate arguments display love and yell at each other for hours until the discourse resolves itself with quick intercourse.

If the feeling of happiness is already inside you, your mind is throwing up barriers to keep you moving past it towards some vital goal. What could that be? Could it be that you have stringent & inflexible rules that advise you when to be happy and how to react to new things?

Millions of people run around, believing that they won't be content until they earn a specific dollar figure or accumulate a nest egg for retirement. The most common monetary goal for Americans is to make $100,000 per year or save one million dollars. This future event is a moment in time, which means that the ambitious will not be pleased until what must be accomplished is achieved.

As surely as the sun breaks the horizon at the dawn's first light, they won't be thrilled when they earn the millions desired because the goal seekers will inevitably rebound to usual moods. All external goals, like possessions or fame, can make us happy for a while, but the familiar turns us around to our everyday states of happiness or despair.

It only takes a few months for a happy person to perceive he won an empty goal. He then will create another dream and unhappily chase the next target. These dream chasers can never be satisfied because they keep postponing joy to get something rumored to make them happy.

Are you skeptical about the idea that wealth and fame will only bring you temporary happiness? I mean, you spent your whole life dreaming of being rich so you could leave all your problems behind.

Wake up to the new reality. Did you not start a new job and feel nervous or excited on the first day? One week later, you felt much more comfortable, blase, and relaxed at work, right?

Or how about learning how to drive and buy your first car? When was the last time you were that excited? Nowadays, you don't think about driving or possessing a vehicle. It's just there on your driveway. It's a beauty, and you still enjoy it, but you don't wake up at dawn excited about having a great car.

You might say gaining wealth or becoming famous is not the same thing as first jobs & new cars. Willing to bet on it? Are you really ready to bet your entire forty-year working life working under miserable conditions to get those five million dollars, that B&B hotel, or corner office partnership? Seriously?

Rebels Strive To Be Their Own Hero

Remarkably successful people overcome this trap by doing what they do for the love of the game. The triumphant desire material markers like cars, mansions and fortunes because it's fun and necessary for lucrative friendships. They also seek internal goals like having beautiful experiences, making loyal friends, and gaining valued skills because becoming your own hero is infinitely more enjoyable than acquiring money and gaining status.

It's our nature; we get excited about new playthings and then lose interest once we have engaged with it for a while. Our minds seek novelty - like new experiences - and we tend to put average things to the side. Wealthy folks take possessions and wealth for granted because the years pass by, and they forget to recognize the value of what they have.

Rebels have a double bind problem should we become wealthy and successful. We may not know chasing external goals like earning money and buying houses will only bring short term pleasure. Until now. Still, many of us have always resisted evolving into that we rebel against - the establishment.

If you grew up in a working-class neighborhood like I did, you probably acquired negative feelings towards our employers and schools, who appeared to be controlling the levers of power. Rich people were the enemy, and our working comrades became the good guys. With maturing eyes, we can see it is not quite that simple.

Once our childish minds chose a team in this battle of reckoned good and evil, our subconscious thoughts decided it would not allow us to switch sides later in life. Some of our innermost views rebel against becoming what we imagine caused us pain, and we will go so far as to wreck our lives to stop the transformation.

So you instinctively know that chasing whatever everyone else is chasing won't make you happy, and you don't want to transform into your 'evil' counterpart. Rebelling against society is a natural and logical response under these circumstances, and figuring out your own way is the best solution.

Actor Bruce Lee fought many conventions against Asian-Americans and battled his own community. Bruce took his martial arts knowledge and combined it with Asian and Western philosophy to create his own fighting style. Inside and out of the ring, he fought to demonstrate that hand combat could be learned by any race.

The Chinese community and Hong Kong elders were displeased and tried to stop him with boycotts, threats, and tournaments. Through bodybuilding and his dedication to his craft, Lee's physical strength made him too tough to beat, and he went on to star in the 'Green Hornet' and 'Enter the Dragon.'

You are right to rebel. And yet, you are wrong to fight back against the desire to express yourself and grow as a person. If you are frustrated and unhappy, you seek both transformation and some sort of enlightenment.

If your mind is resisting change, it will give you frightening thoughts that keep you stuck in the past. Being stuck is like living in a cage. No living creature wants to be caged in. Yet here you are. Stuck.

Separating Invented Thoughts From Genuine Facts Is Impossible

You are not your thoughts. They are the software to the hardware that is your mind. Your thoughts are full of good and bad ideas that are keeping you stuck in your present reality. You can replace any and all disempowering thoughts with new versions that you no longer want to fight against.

Have you considered that your resistance to all the goals and dreams in your head means that your soul does not accept them as your own and asks you to keep looking? Money could be the thing that gets you to what you really want, and not the primary goal in itself.

Do not believe everything you hear. Sometimes your thoughts represent reality, but sometimes they are just thoughts. Look outside your window. That tree you see is a thought in your head. It is real. Now humor me and picture a giant pink elephant sitting in the branches. He is smiling at you. Can you see it?

That is a thought, but it is not real. It's only imaginary. I believe that many beliefs in your head are invented rather than absolute.

Some are true, and some are false. Could your assumptions about your wretchedness be as authentic as your pink elephant sitting in a tree? Other people gave you ideas, and you accepted them as genuine without questioning it. Please stop doing that!

Realize that most of us had limited exposure to the possibilities of the world in our upbringing. We learned from our parents, friends, teachers, and media a fraction of the knowledge that was out there.

Some tribesmen have never seen an airplane or touched a computer. Your life is beyond their reality. As sophisticated as you are, there are realities you have no idea about. You have only explored the tip of the iceberg of what is available to you. There are neighborhoods, cities, and nations experiencing events and traditions that we had no idea existed. We still don't know what is out there.

What if others tell you things to be happy might be wrong? What if the programs of happiness work for the majority of people but won't work for you? It is time you explore more of the world and find out something that draws you in rather than forces you to rebel against it.

I bet you think far too much. I know it! Thinking is private and safe because nobody can see your thoughts, and you can keep everything a secret. But your plans are limited, causing you to unintentionally walk around in circles in your mind. If your negative thoughts overwhelm your positivity and repeat them each day, you probably won't escape your unhappiness.

Challenge 12 - It's time to take action and explore more of the world. Can you take online classes on Udemy.com or Skillshare.com that you never took before? Could you go to networking meetings in industries that you are interested in participating in?

Yes, you are now exposed, and what you think about is revealed in your actions. Friends might sway, mock, and tease you from dawn to dusk. It's none of their business. Have faith you will find new friends in whatever endeavor you find passion in.

Whatever you try will benefit you. Even if you fail or dislike it, the experience of trying it will add to your memories and stories. You will become more attractive to others. If people ask about something you tried, you can pass on information that can help them. With every attempt, you may get closer and closer to that which sets your heart afire.

NOTES

CHAPTER 13

Rebels Avoid Success by Hiding Behind Addictions

It is easier for the Rebel personality to get addicted to mood-altering substances or behaviors than others because we are desperate to escape life's dull mundanity. What ordinary people run towards, we run away from. This unusual behavior takes us to a lonely place where we fill it with alcohol, drugs, and other compulsive pleasures.

Addiction is defined as the continued use of a mood-altering substance or behavior despite adverse consequences—people who fear success self-sabotage by indulging in their pleasurable habits. Achieving something meaningful is not easy. Enjoying the harmful pleasures of life is. It feels so good to avoid dealing with the problems you can get addicted to substances that keep you from undertaking the discomfort of attaining greatness.

As compulsive thinkers, running our minds in a loop of the same fears, memories, and fantasies day after day, we avoid the present moment. We sleepwalk through our lives in a disorganized, unimaginative way, following the crowd, experiencing what our friends are going through, each searching for what we can't find.

We are easy prey for drug dealers, alcohol stores, bars, clubs, and gambling establishments because they just need to tap into our need to revolt against society. Once we know it's against the law, we want it. But we don't really want to skate on thin ice to break the law or become outcasts. What we really desire is revolution and transformation.

You might remember it, that first snort of cocaine, that first win at blackjack, that fantastic night drinking. Whatever happened to you, this experience was inversely superior to your mundane life, and you wanted more.

Suddenly one day, you experience something that gives an intense shot of pleasure to your brain. You have entered nirvana through artificial means and temporarily shut off that annoying critical inner voice in your head.

Some problems just creep up on you. As a teen, perhaps you felt more relaxed and confident when you smoked or drank with your friends. Then you smoked another or chugged one more until you could not stop. Maybe you started on more stimulating drugs or switched to harder liquor in your late teens.

Why not? There were so many people encouraging us to participate. "He's cool. He can handle his liquor." or "She is alright. She gives me smokes from time to time." Maybe our friends knew their limits when it was time to go home and sleep, but we could not cease or find alternative ways to cope with life.

Suitable for peer pressure, those with rebellious tendencies can easily fall into addictive behavior. We need to fit in somewhere, and rebels tend to stick together. You get two kids who hate an icy world frosty to their ambitions, and they will find foolish ways to distract themselves.

Most recovering addicts will claim they don't know what happened. One moment they were okay, and then they were a mess. 'I was not thinking clearly,' they claim. But they were. They were thinking before, during, and after each episode. Victims knew it was happening to them, but they just could not stop - they could only watch themselves self-destruct over time.

The highs of enjoying the addiction become normal and what used to be normal becomes harder to tolerate in comparison. As the habit gets more substantial, the pressure to run away from the inner critical voice becomes more intense, and most people can't help but run back to their addictions.

Interventions don't work that well for rebels. We hate being told what to do. Telling us that we can't have something wrong for us makes us want it even more. The fighter fights against everything unless the former addict learns how to love and enjoy new alternatives.

Howard Schultz's love of coffee and his tendency to fight against norms helped Starbucks grow from sixty shops to twenty-one thousand stores in sixty-five countries. This poor kid who grew up in the projects of Brooklyn, New York, proved his critics wrong. Schultz's compulsion as CEO to growing Starbucks helped fuel America's growing addiction to 'take out and drive through' fancy coffee.

Schultz, like other successful people, focused all his energy on building the culture of his company. Most addicts usually don't have a dream big that it distracts them from repetitive pleasure-seeking or a purpose that won't come off the rails when difficulties strike.

If a rich and famous celebrity falls into addiction after achieving success, it usually means their passions no longer have the emotional resonance to keep them moving forward. They lost their zest, and it hurts so bad to lose their reason for being, they have to numb their pain with drinking, drugs, sex, or whatever takes them out of their suffering.

Most addicts become a slave to their desires, and their lives fall out of balance. All their efforts are geared to feeding their hunger in response to the emptiness inside all of us. Their destination is the same - a crash, recovery, or death.

We rely on social cues to make decisions, and watching groups of people working towards a successful common purpose is very empowering. One reason AA (Alcoholics Anonymous) works is everyone is pulling together in harmony. When an addict has acknowledged he has hit rock bottom and wants to change, his mind is full of self-defeating habits. He must freely rely on others to lead him out until he can establish healthier alternative behavior patterns.

Our minds like the familiar and will fight uncomfortable changes even if it's good for us. Addiction can be beaten with action (not thinking). Recovery is slow, but it also took years to hit bottom too. Compulsive thinking got us into trouble, so avoiding overthinking may be the best approach.

Some psychotherapists use 'paradoxical intervention' with patients by prescribing the behavior that needs changing. For example, they tell their patients with anger issues to yell, scream, and lose their temper, and the patients do so until it becomes an unpleasant experience for them. Then the patients don't want to do it anymore.

I heard this story where some parents caught their fourteen-year-old son smoking a cigarette, so they sat him down in the kitchen and made him smoke a whole pack all at once—twenty cigarettes in a row over a couple of hours. Of course, he turned green and puked his guts out. This awful feeling of associating cigarettes with throwing up was now anchored in his brain, and the kid never smoked again. I don't know if such discipline is legal today.

People can't solve their problems without creating an empty space in their lives full of pain. This must be temporary. If an addict succeeded in getting rid of their problem but did not replace it with something else equally pleasurable, they will slide back like an ice skater stumbling to stay afoot into long-standing addictions.

Quite a few choose the victim mode of being. They believe others have ruined their lives and want to be rescued time and time again. The parent, lover, or friend who falls for such trickery messes up their lives as well. They are frequently on call to pick up the addict or get them out of financial messes. It's only when everyone walks away, and the victim hits rock bottom, they realize their addiction has cost them everything.

Challenge 13 - Rebels need to revolt against rebelling to change their ways. When you make the addiction the enemy, now we have something to fight against—weed, booze, smokes, casinos, stealing.

Forgive yourself for your addictions because these were the lubricants you found helped you fit into a world that did not accept you fully. Your habits are the problems we can push against, and becoming clean is our act of defiance.

But quitting has to be an idea that originates in our minds. If anyone commands that we terminate our addictions, we will happily engage in that conflict and continue to screw up our lives in insubordination. No, we must conclude that it was not our fault & that our addictions will ruin us.

NOTES

CHAPTER 14

Confidence Follows The

Attempt, Not Before

Most confidence you witness is as real as snow flurries - it looks like real snow but melts as quickly as it arrives. Some people seem sure of themselves, but you quickly discover authenticity when you question their depth of knowledge: parrots, the lot of them. Copying and repeating the simple ideas they like and rejecting vast amounts of wisdom because to do so would crack the veneer of their puffed up self-esteem.

There is one advantage of lacking false conviction. Not burdened by the feeling of overconfidence, tentative seekers will approach with caution, asking around to gain certainty. This philosophy towards experimenting may increase, not decrease, the chance of their success.

But caution only works when we have enough confidence to get started. A spirit that lives at rock bottom is not the state of mind you want to be in.

We, the modest, also overestimate the strengths of others and underestimate what we can accomplish ourselves. People watching reveals a lot - most people claim they feel confident most of the time, but their body language tells otherwise. They try to protect their self-identity by pretending to have it all, but their slouched shoulders and anxious eyes show they are not.

Many don't recognize false confidence as the norm. The insecure walk around thinking that everyone appears to be assured, so why not me? In truth, crowds become nervous about strange things, and they only display confidence inside their tiny comfort zone.

By remaining in their safe place, they boldly hide their flaws and pretend to be something they are not. Our society has taught us to think that way to survive, and very few questions about why we behave the way we do. On the rare occasion they step outside their comfort zone, people temporarily lose their confidence until they get their bearings. Then their comfort zone expands, and their world grows a little larger.

Are you sure about your jobs but nervous during parties, or are you among those who enjoy spending time with families but don't feel confident at work? Maybe you are satisfied at work, play, and families, yet lose confidence in new situations like rock climbing or public speaking?

If everyone knew each other's 'crap' they would not be so intimidated by those they admire. When friendships are more comfortable with people with different backgrounds, heritages, and talents, we can learn from each other and overcome more problems than society is undertaking.

You don't fit into the norm. The average is not for you. Resistance is in the blood, so it may take years to determine your purpose. Living in uncertainty requires a person to search in places they have not been before, and this may cause more incredible feelings of doubt than someone who settles for what is expedient.

Gain Strength Through Vulnerability

I think you should seek experiences that make you feel less confident, not more. Yes, you read that right. Step into jobs and situations that make your knees shake and give you heartaches because you will feel much healthier after your transformation. Who has the last laugh when you can do that which others fear to try?

In the short term, you will experience far more fear than those who hide from their problems. In the long term, faith allows you to move forward with even bigger goals, while those lacking in spirit are still battling their same mental fears or worries every day.

When you see the situation or person is not quite like you imagined it to be, your beliefs can shatter, like recognizing the downpour of flurries is not the beginnings of a snowstorm. This creative mind you possess creates demon dogs out of poodles. Your deep false beliefs might need to be desensitized through repeated exposure so you can mature into the person you dreamed of becoming.

Confidence comes from taking action in the present moment, rather than thinking about trying in the future. The key is to be your own drill sergeant. Many wish something would change in their lives from outside themselves. They are waiting to be given marching orders. But no outsider is going to save them from what is going on inside their heads.

Our fear of success reduces our confidence, and your lack of courage builds up our fear of success. The older you get, the stronger your fears grow and more your trust erodes. When we stop believing in ourselves, we magnify our weaknesses and discount our strengths, and so the world required to achieve success will look like a mountain instead of the hill it really is.

We have a cycle of confidence that is a continuous loop of thinking, doing, and feeling. For example, if a guy thinks he can't get a date, he won't take action; he will feel bad about it, reinforcing his thinking to not accept future action and continue to feel terrible about it.

You can break this cycle in any of the three stages of thinking, doing, and feeling and turn it around so that your new thoughts make you feel fearless to take optimistic actions.

We are imitators, for the most part, not innovators. It's safer to let someone else stick his head out and takes all the risks. But when these risks pay off, the rewards and glory go to the leader who had the confidence to go first.

I believe what you really are after is not confidence in specific things like public speaking, paragliding, and dancing, but having that general disposition of those who are relaxed no matter the situation. One of those people who acts like everything is going to be alright.

 Even if they fail, they will rise and try again tomorrow. The brave might feel nervous in certain situations and have their share of setbacks, but overall they are winners and expect to keep winning.

Be Brave Like Excitable Children

With the surety of young children, six-year-old Ryan Hreljac stepped forward to help. He learned that children in Africa had to walk long distances searching for freshwater to cook & clean with when they should be in school. Ryan did not have the doubts and insecurities of adults to stop him from helping these children.

After fundraising and speaking out about the cause, Ryan's first well was built in 1999 at the Angolo Primary School in a northern

Ugandan village. His determination led Ryan's Well Foundation to complete more than nine hundred projects worldwide, bringing access to clean water and sanitation to nearly a million people.

Imagine if we could take children's nativity and innocence to start projects without fear and mix in the wisdom and skills of parents to see them to completion? How many more Ryans exist, but the parents or teachers discouraged them because the adults lacked faith in the universe's bounty?

As a society, we can only rise to our leaders' highest confidence level and no higher. We don't see how managers take action, how officers fight adversity, how leaders succeed, and how directors fail. We only see superstars' results after years of struggle and think, "that is not me. I don't have those special skills." We don't realize the most compelling stories of heroism require deleting all the details that reveal our shared humanity.

Challenge 14 - Confidence is something that takes time to acquire. There are no overnight successes. When you do something repeatedly (like playing guitar or driving a car), it becomes part of your subconscious mind. You can do the familiar without concentrating or worrying, and this makes you seem confident.

Is there something you can do to build confidence in yourself that is repetitive, challenging, and enjoyable? Not video games or social media. That's too easy. How about handwriting classes where you learn how to write interesting short stories? What about dance classes with increasingly intricate moves? Maybe learn how to shoot basketball hoops properly, so you improve your free throw percentage?

When you learn new things, you gain specific confidence in that skill. As you acquire new skills, you also gain a strong sense of self-confidence to handle new challenges. Most people don't have this priceless feeling as they age, and they are spiritually impoverished from living in fear of the unknown.

NOTES

CHAPTER 15

Friends Come & Go, But

Personality Is Forever

It is not easy having a personality that fights ideas before we accept them. But then who are we to complain? It might surprise you to discover that others secretly admire your creative thinking, spontaneous nature, and independent mind. People who know us feel jealous that we can be free spirits who ignore the rules that contain them and play on the edge of danger.

Ordinary followers desire our free-spirited constitution as an antidote to their conformity. But if they only knew the inner turmoil inside as we strive to determine which rules to conform to and which orders to bend.

Many rebels self-destruct and inadvertently choose addiction and poverty in the struggle to understand who they really are. They don't know how to thrive in a society that tries to contain outliers.

Good Friends Allow Us To Be Artists & Revolutionaries

We can't be contained in the boxes others try to put us in. We are the artists, revolutionists, inventors, and philosophers, which makes us a threat to the status quo. We are the moonlight that paves the way when the sky turns black, and the illumination from our art allows others to see what was invisible to them before.

Current Western culture gives many freedoms to experiment and express ourselves because the elite believes they can exploit the riches that come from our minds. We should not take these freedoms for granted forever once the powerful observe no value in affording us these liberties.

Simon Bolivar was a divisive military and political leader who split from the loyalist autocracy and gained many allies when several Latin American countries revolted against the King. Achieving independence from the Spanish Empire meant risking violent death in battle or by execution.

Bolivar also served as president from 1819 to 1830 of Gran Colombia (current day Columbia, Ecuador, Venezuela, and Panama). To fight to lead his people to the earliest democracies meant being caught up in the arguments and conflicts of supporters who disagreed with his policies. President Bolivar chose to be a strong leader of principle rather than a people pleaser.

Strong of will, friends, and neighbors don't know what to make of our unpredictable behavior. If they are deeply conservative, they may even find us flawed characters, not worthy of consideration. Some are tolerant of our youthful indiscretions but urge us to grow up and settle for the ordinary after age thirty.

Artists with rebellious tendencies tend to congregate at the lower end of the social stratosphere. The starving artist myth is partly true because the very best in their field are richly rewarded while the amateur is ignored. We also try many things, fail, and quit before they can bear fruit. Our contemptuousness and impatience get the best of us.

Many have difficulty making friends with people who are above and below them on the status hierarchy. Your suspicions are correct. Some of your current friends will not be able to handle your new-found success, should you find it. Life becomes more formidable than it should be because we have to manage all the good and bad relationships around us.

It's All Fun & Games Until You Break Something

Some relationships only work well if you are just messing around and having fun. Once you grow as a person, their own insecurities will show up, and they will become more critical than any impartial stranger you will face. Fortunately, as you develop more social and technical skills, you will gather new friends who can raise you up to higher levels and keep old allies who still see great fun within your character.

Your friends and family are negative because they are fearful of rejection by others. The majority of us conform to the conservative ideal of how we should act to not get booted out of our groups. Our friends become jealous and frustrated because they can't break out of their conformity while we are getting or becoming what they want for themselves.

We enjoy the peace of adapting to our chosen group and belonging to a circle of friends- it is good to take a break from fighting the world. Yet even within rebel societies, many people feel the loss of their own identity with the group and are afraid to disagree with others.

What bothers me the most is this fear of not fitting in causes us to walk around in a suit of emotional armor. Our guard is always up, and our authentic self is cloaked the same as overcast clouds concealing the glow of the moon.

It is harder to make friends when you have to maintain your image, and they have to retain theirs. If two people of different ethnic, ages, and economic groups pass each other, they could observe physical differences, ignore abstract commonalities, and avoid breaching the possibility of friendship.

When people can't have real honest communication, it causes second-guessing, and many friendships fail to get off the ground. We also can see that some people are in a state of constant anxiety as they worry about the strength of the relationship and fear the loss of companionship.

Rebellion Is A Lonely State Of Being

Loneliness is a real distraction. When you lack meaningful connections, there is a part of your restless spirit that won't stay silent and concentrate on achieving your cumulative goals. Those with a restless spirit either move from one shallow relationship to another or spend a tremendous amount of effort trying to maintain their current unstable relationships.

Detachment is a good signal from your body to your mind of the disconnect you feel when you are not in harmony with others. So you want more friendships or deeper ones, or a romantic partner, right? And you don't have these relationships, or you do, but they are superficial at best? Our loneliness tells us to end this isolation and seek better human connections with those who will allow us to be our true selves.

Everyone feels lonely sometimes, and we try to distract ourselves with materialism and pleasure-seeking to mask our loneliness. Many people have settled into unsatisfying relationships that last for years, just to numb the feeling.

Countless people are in relationships that do not satisfy them, but they do not attempt to leave since they find it a heartbreaking challenge to find a more compatible partner. The emotional guards we construct over the years are like clouds expanding into the fog, obscuring the sunlight, the person we really are.

When relationships end badly or just die out, the people involved may move on quickly. Still, you could spend months and years dwelling on their past if you don't—the emotional stabs of harsh words, the disappointments of love lost and repeated replaying arguments.

Two friends may spend time with each other in a gossipy superficial way and not reveal or learn their true identity for many years. Each has a false belief that showing their flaws or real interests may cause them to lose social status with the friend.

This culture, which promotes certain status-seeking behaviors, creates a situation where supposed friends may really be enemies, and perceived enemies should be friends. The more wealth and fame we have, the more likely people may gravitate to us to take advantage of us, and it becomes harder to decide who is our true friend and who is not.

Most leaders are afraid to make dramatic changes, even if it's for the benefit of the greater good. Their instinctual self-preservation (a hard motivation) overrides their desire to help others outside their family and close friends (a soft motivation).

Challenge 15 - Our prejudging of people stops us from getting to know them, and then we tend to stick to those who are familiar and safe. The need to maintain our public personality and hide our true self keeps us from reaching connections with those we know at the superficial level.

If we did not create these false barriers and public identities to hide our true natures, we would find it easier to have genuine connections with others. It is a rare friend or parent who teaches how to interact with others in a way that allows our best characteristics to shine through without causing offense to those with different values.

Just like we need to feed ourselves when hungry, we must resolve our lonely feelings through fulfilling connections. Hopefully, you have a best friend or two you admire and like. What traits or characteristics do they possess that you feel grateful for? Are they a good listener? Do they know how to make you laugh? Are they reliable?

Think of their qualities and then think of acquaintances who might have similar traits. Maybe you can cultivate deeper relationships by spending more time gaining the trust of strangers and building up your social circle in surprising experimentation?

NOTES

CHAPTER 16

Confused? Great!

Are you like everyone else? - wandering around in a state of confusion from unlimited choices. A force of nature like a tornado ripping through cornfields, we of the rebellious ilk want to change established norms even if it means breaking things at first. Our primary impediment is that we have difficulty making the commitments to put such plans into action.

It is against the rebel's nature to imitate the average. We would like to be extraordinary, or at the minimum, unique in what we do. But what if you are surrounded by people who live everyday lives, and you ache for more than the ordinary?

Should you choose an extra challenging course, you will be required to undertake your own path untraveled by your friends and family and seek guidance from wary strangers who have persisted before you.

I see no other option but ditching the familiar for the unknown. Taking a new approach requires you to shut off your cutting internal voice and step into valleys of doubt and forests of uncertainty that raises the probability you won't comprehend what is happening to you. Well, at least in the beginning.

I am sorry that you must step into perplexing circumstances to get where you are going. You have to become comfortable with being in a state where you don't have all the answers. To get a sense of clarity of who you are and what truly makes you happy requires knocking on doors & exploring strange nooks and crannies.

A new venture is a frightening place to you at first - just like a twister took Dorthy to the land of Oz- you have to feel your way around and seize unexpected opportunities to find out what works best for you. Ordinary people don't try new ideas because they are afraid to try and appear foolish.

Everyone, even Navy Seals, UFC fighters & CEOs, are fearful of something. Like millions before you, are you holding back fears by avoiding situations that trigger your anxiety? Can you join those mysterious communities who, strangely, run towards personalities and practices that frighten the rest of us?

Our fear of living mediocre and unsatisfying lives is more public than our fear of failing, so we step forward into tempered anarchy. Overachievers, like you, are so apprehensive of missing out and not reaching their ends they won't stop until they get what they want.

Most subversive thinkers had to take calculated, even dangerous, risks to escape their predicament. Did you know in the quest to spread Kentucky Fried Chicken franchises across America, Colonel Sanders, age 65, began by driving from town to town, offering to sell his secret chicken recipe of 11 herbs and spices? Sitting at home, living on social security was not an option for Mr. Sanders, so he punched the road and never looked back.

When you are a person who develops a strong sense of identity after exploring much of what life has to offer, you may look back at your former shallow self in admiration. Miraculously, through divine guidance, you made the right choices despite a lack of reliable information.

To take full advantage of appreciating life's journey, you should be sensitive to trying new things and avoiding prejudging activities negatively before you attempt them. Others may find this behavior confusing, as they desire to limit themselves to what is expected.

Judging Opportunities Quickly & Recklessly Increases Confusion

See, if you live in a world where you judge circumstances and people as good or bad (clearly black or white) before you experience it fully, you are confining yourself to reject most of everything before deciding whether it will benefit you or not.

Most of the 1,008 restaurant owners who refused Colonel Harlan Sanders's famous chicken recipe could not imagine how they could make more money selling his special dish than their prized family recipe. Sanders slept in his car and spun like an unstoppable twister for months, living off his chicken samples, until he found a partner willing to take a chance.

Make no mistake. You probably behave more like the thousand restaurateurs who rejected a golden opportunity than Harland Sanders. To reverse this behavior, you must learn to suspend your prejudices against possibilities until you acquire superior facts about your reality. You are judging situations and details from previous information gifted to you by ordinary folk who neglected to search for definitive answers.

The average may push you or encourage you to join their mode of thinking, but you know better than that. Your tendency to fight what feels wrong causes conflict or resistance between your family but surrender goes against your more considerate nature.

Your past controls you more than you realize. If you risked something once and loved it, your feelings permit you to seek that activity again. If you notice something similar but not exactly what you experienced in the past, you will likely shortcut it— bypass prejudging it to be negative and say yes to it anew.

My mind functions to learn by comparing new stuff with items I am familiar with. So do you. Is this a survival instinct or a learned response from our parents? I don't know.

Why do we tend to identify and assess everything before we have all the facts? Our natural inclination is to make quick split-second decisions and label everything we encounter into one of two categories. Either it is harmful & we avoid it, or it is safe, and we use it.

The downside is you may make snap judgments on experiences that are not well-known or reject things that fill you with unpleasant memories. You can recognize the dilemma with labeling things quickly? Those who have a history of abuse, pain, and unhappiness will likely be very cautious about enduring new things. At the same time, those with joyous childhoods will probably welcome a wide variety of experiences.

Rebels Have Thicker Skin In Confusing Situations

Most will not venture into the unknown for fear of loss of reputation. Ordinary people can be persuaded by guilt, shame, influence, and manipulation to stick with the program. The polite society holds it is bad manners to go against obligations and create conflict to keep allies accountable. Working people are too intimidated to speak out in public and offer solutions that contradict norms. Can you see why the meek are too frightened to inherit the world?

Revolutionary thinkers want to teach those who are not rebels how to see past their fears and distrust as chains of bondage that constrain them from success. When everyone starts to communicate openly and honestly, the confusion will end, and more will get what they want.

I am asking you to reconsider the dominant worldview that automatically judges people, places, and things as either good or evil. Morality and decision making is on a sliding scale composed of a thousand shades of gray. There are countless viewpoints on many topics, many of which are incorrect.

For example, lying that a relative is not in your home might be kind of immoral, but it might be appropriate to save a life or prevent theft & violence. The same lie becomes highly unethical if you shield a fugitive who will share the spoils of future crimes with you.

An eighty-year-old might see a forty-year-old as youthful, while a fifteen-year-old may see the middle-aged person as ancient. That middle-aged person might see his life as almost over, or he might think he has barely started to live. If you believe there is a magic formula to comprehend which idea is safe and which is dangerous, you will spend your whole existence searching in vain. Nobody has figured it out yet.

Life is very messy. And people try to label others, prejudge them, put them in boxes to organize this chaos in their heads. We are doing it all wrong. People cannot see past what they see in their heads. If they don't communicate with people who are different from themselves, they can't dislodge those first impressions from childhood.

Your judgment is as likely to be mistaken as it is right. If you notice something and describe it the way you perceive it, the odds say that you will be wildly inaccurate in your report. How can you? You are guessing based on your personal and limited history of exposure.

Standards & Principles Break Through States of Confusion

So why are you confused? You don't have a system of sorting, experiencing, and judging events and people in your life because you don't have standards, values, or guiding principles. If you don't have something to stand for, you may fall for anything.

Do you want to be a puppet on a string, performing whatever someone manipulative and intelligent wants you to do? Do you want to be sucked into the vortex of the social media tornado that turns friend against friend and brother against sister because we perceive ideologies in a different light?

Unlike many conformists, you have devised unique principles that stabilize your decision making. For one, Rebels dislike making commitments that don't feel right. We are not persuaded by obligations or reputation, guilt, or manners, norms, conformity. We make our own rules, and we have to stand by them to develop a system for judging things.

For example, if you feel honesty and integrity are of high value for you to live up to, you won't tolerate situations and people who bring dishonesty into your life. There is no confusion about that at all. You don't have to decide should I break the law here or should I steal there. It's no longer negotiable. Your personal rules help you decide whether to oblige others or revolt against the pressure they place on you to comply.

Systems disrupt confusion and bring order to chaos. You are in charge of your own life when you can process the sensory data (stories, music & news heard, seen, touched, tasted & smelled) through your own principles and code of conduct, not the ideology your community mindlessly serves.

If you are bewildered by failing governing and bureaucratic systems, it is because you have the intuition to recognize what others cannot. The world is organized turmoil. Maybe we should not blindly accept things like capitalism, socialism, feminism, atheism, humanism, and the hundreds of other belief systems as the only solution to global problems. Can you think for yourself, so others don't do it for you?

Billions live their lives, trying to survive, and it's a wonder we get through the day without cheating, stealing, or punching one another. To keep everything from falling apart, we must lie to ourselves that everything is okay. But it's not okay.

There are millions of problems and opportunities to fix what is wrong with the world. You desire not to conform, break norms, and change values because you can feel that something is not quite right with how things are operating. It is in you to help bring order to this chaos.

You can perceive that billions are stumbling around lost, looking for leadership, unsure because they do not live by standards, principles, ethics, and codes of honor that suit their particular life choices. Can you find something you genuinely believe in so that you can help others find their way?

Challenge 16 - You are different and are tough enough to make changes, try new things, and bring about revolutions. If you are not going to seek the burden of leadership, then who will? Even if you don't aspire to lead others, you need to take charge of yourself.

To do this, you should list all materials available to you to succeed. Express gratitude for your home, car, computer, books, college education, and teachers because acknowledging their value helps you draw more utility from them.

Why not create a regular monthly habit to detail all those personalities, objects, and tools you can locate? Why are you grateful for all these people and things?

NOTES

CHAPTER 17

Guilt Is A Weapon & A Shield

Just as the pounding surf knocked us off our feet, others have shifted waves of guilt to mold us at our expense. No more! Today can be the day we seize this weapon of manipulation from those frienemies in our social circle and use it to shape our worlds for our benefit rather than enrich others.

Rebels are not exempt from our humanity. We feel some semblance of guilt when we disobey orders, procrastination, or don't produce our fair share. Aware we broke a moral or work standard that should have been upheld, our belief systems protest this violation with feelings of guilt, shame, anxiety, and worry.

Radicals know we should have done what was expected of us, yet we do the opposite because nothing overrides our core belief that "nobody tells us what to do."

Guilt tactics can be a decisive driving force for the construction of a more satisfying life. Many successful executives and professionals have benefited financially because their parents provoked guilty feelings whenever they failed to study, make the honors list, and achieve the parent's goals. Calling people out on their obligations works wonders, and many practices guilting as a shortcut to take what they desire.

Unfortunately, those of us with a rebellious nature are somewhat immune to the feelings of guilt. Try all you want to manipulate us; if we don't want to do something, we won't do it. Something instinctual inside a rebel tells them to challenge influences imposed on them.

Still, when we don't have more effective approaches than our parents & teachers, radicals can stagnate in a morose feeling of alienation and nihilism.

Guilt Makes For A Superior Life

Guilt can be an asset when you align your thoughts with your real life's purpose. The disgrace of not fulfilling the obligations you choose will override the shaming techniques manipulative people will try on you. For example, when you have responsibilities to other people who depend on you, your guilt will keep you to your duties even when you desire to play hooky in the stadium, bars, or mall.

Guilt only goes so far. Once we have achieved the expectations of those delivering shameful feelings, we will quit if we lack the internal motivation to continue. That is one advantage a personality who fights the system has over civilians who live by others' expectations. Their internal motivation will sustain the activity so long as there is a belief in the cause.

Marie Curie, a Polish scientist of the early 20th century, was a real rebel because she did not accept the whisperings of polite society that guilted women to be subordinate to their husbands. Her willfulness was so strong that she continued her research into old age. Only radiation poisoning at age sixty-six could stop Marie.

Marie Curie subverted expectations by channeling her ceaseless curiosity and passionate exploration into scientific research, discovering polonium, radium, the X-Ray, and winning the Nobel prize in 1903. With the support of her husband, Pierre Curie, and other physicists, she fought for her education, learning in secret in Poland and gaining a graduate degree at the University of Paris.

By ignoring expectations & blocking shaming tactics, her higher ideals towards advancing science were far greater than any notions of women's role in society. With this inspirational story in mind, what is the WHY bigger than the guilt ruling you?

I must warn you that while returning to the righteous path may relieve internal feelings of guilt on your part, companions might employ more heinous uses of coercion to keep you in line.

Most ordinary people can't understand us and often don't like what we do with good reason. We can be uncooperative and inconsiderate - stuck in our heads with our ongoing battles of whether to obey or disobey, we often don't see that we are losing friends and allies who have had enough.

Success requires change, and unless the people in our lives can accept the change in us, they will blame you for fostering growth in their own world. Don't be fooled by the seemingly high intelligence around you; even shrewd teachers often dislike change for the better.

When blaming other people for holding us back, we must take some of the blame ourselves. It is not necessarily the error, the criticism, and demands of others blocking us -it's how we interpret and respond to others that are cursing us to feel guilty.

Some taste success and then self-destruct through addictive behaviors and other self-imposed punishment, all in the attempt to bury the feeling of guilt. Ignoring guilty feelings as an emotion is hard to erase because it is cloaked inside childhood memories. It's challenging to modify behaviors learned before preschool.

It's also a mental exercise in futility - guilty feelings bring up past memories of guilty behaviors, which brings us more blameworthy emotions. Your subconscious mind is trying to keep you compulsively pondering so that you lose vital energy for risk-taking and finally give up.

Please don't even try to fight back. An easier way is to reduce your shameful feelings by making smart life choices aligned with your own values. Find a goal or dream worthy of your attention, and obligations imposed by others will fade into background noise.

When you let others impose guilt on you, and it works, you have taught them to continue using this behavior. If the people in your life love and respect you, they will give you the space to chase your dream. Maybe not at first, but sooner or later, they will come around. You must do what is right for you and not what is popular or cool.

It is inescapable. People will try to make you feel guilty to alter your behavior because they have seen this manipulation work on other people. Most of the time, negative influences are like the pounding surf thumping you off your surfboard because most personalities do not want you to surpass them.

Even if you had a weak disposition that cracked under pressure, there are many types of people in our lives, all with competing demands, and we could fill our days and nights trying to meet their ever-growing expectations. We will never completely get rid of the feelings of guilt that we could be doing more.

There are plenty of narcissistic friends and relatives who only seem happy if you have to give up everything for them. Most caring people don't desire to participate in relationships where you are suffering from their demands. You must combat the selfishness of those who don't care about you with your own self-regard.

Revolutionaries Are Greater Than Minor Obligations

It's your life. You must chase your own goals. No one can't make other people feel happy because humans are fickle and unpredictable. Only they can satisfy themselves. What if you realize you are self-sacrificing your desires for others, and they are still not fulfilled? Would you continue for no reason?

Maybe guilt and shame work on some rebels because it's an escape from the inner conflicts within? We cling to distractions, addictions, and mindless tasks as drowning sailors reach for life preservers in the waves. While we are restless for evolution to happen, we also resist the very change we desire. How crazy is that?

Businesses and managers are always changing something or other, and we are often the last to comply even if we agree with the correction. Rebels act like we are above the rules unless we create the customs ourselves. Even then, we might break our own rules. I don't blame other people for being befuddled and confused by us; we can't understand ourselves either.

As we struggle with routines and daily tasks that we despise, bosses, teachers, and parents get frustrated. Why can't we do what we are told? Why don't we feel liable for missing deadlines and breaking other rules they hold so dear?

Subversives don't accept the guilt imposed by non-rebels because we prioritize our freedom and independence higher than mundane demands. Our principles neutralize their actions, just as sandy beaches absorb the force of the oceans' waves.

While we may rebel against the mundane and routine, Rebels love principles of honesty and authenticity. We desire the self-determination to find truth and justice in a world full of funhouse mirrors of exceptions and double talk. When we violate the more essential principles of the world, we are trying to construct, our hearts' shameful burning of guilt penetrates our consciousness and resolves to do better.

If you rebelliously disregard the guilt issued by others, you won't internalize it in your subconscious and can surf on top of these waves of influence instead of being drowned by shame. What an immeasurable quality of courage you possess when you check shaming techniques and crave something more extraordinary than what your circle of friends and family believe you are capable of!

Challenge 17 - This goes back to finding your ultimate WHY. Why are you here on planet earth? What is your purpose? Can you find something that drives you like a tsunami so that you feel terrible pangs of regret if you abandon your cause? Once you design your main reasoning for being, you can leverage yourself to find the power your dark side wants to keep hidden. Now you have taken your control back.

As forgetful creatures, we are more appreciative when keeping them in mind and will utilize objects, opportunities & people further than what we take for granted.

NOTES

CHAPTER 18

Find the 'Why' Behind Your Purpose

You are rebellious in nature. So many popular ideas don't appeal to you. With every thread of your being, you are saying NO to most of what is presented to you. You respond, "I do not desire those objects and wishes of which my friends and family say I should pursue. You can't make me do whatever I don't want to do."

Listen up. You are a dangerous weapon that can disrupt the forces that are troubling your family and community. Others can't rebel like you do. They are bound by their upbringing and personality to conform and obey. Don't take this for granted - it's your gift and your curse.

To deny your rebellious nature is to dismiss that inner intelligence which could make you great. It will never go away. This is not a phase of teenage angst; you demand to go on a solitary path because you must. You could choose to go with the crowd and fit in, never saying a word that could offend, and you will have failed your purpose.

The harsh reality is that other than your parents & spouse, you are the only person who cares about developing yourself. Nobody else worries whether you win or lose unless it affects them negatively. Friends and family want you to acquire success if it's to their benefit but could potentially obstruct you if they don't understand what you are up to. Relax, that's human nature. Most of us behave this way.

Think Different To Be Different.

Unsuccessful in your latest challenge, you probably muse similar thoughts as those who failed before you. Does it comfort you to know there are millions of people who are fighting battles in their own heads, just like you? I did not think so. Wouldn't you rather win than hang out with crowds going in the wrong direction?

Doing nothing is not an option. You receive minimal benefit from choosing to opt-out of decision making. Maybe you can live like that, relying on the generosity of others to do your thinking for you, but I can't. You must learn how to become a decision-making machine...

If you want to make better decisions, can I suggest you attempt gaining more experience executing bad judgments? Yes, you should seek to explore more of the world to discover your particular shade of rebelliousness. But rebels don't want instruction or orders; we ache for information and guidance. Let us do it our way, and we will be fine.

A return to experiential learning to find your 'Why' is absolutely necessary because the thoughts of writers won't be sufficient. Did you learn how to ride a bike by writing a paper about it, doing research, thinking it through, wondering about the consequences of failing, dreaming about it? No one learns how to ride unless they step outside and get on that bicycle.

You saw your brother, sister, or friends riding their bikes, and your envious feelings urged you to beg your parents for a new bike. They were having fun, and you were not. So you got on your training bike and forced yourself to stay on until you found your balance. Failure was not an option.

Our patterns of success or failure are mainly rooted in proof of concept. We had to see others fly a plane before we did it ourselves, we observed someone else lift two hundred lbs before we tried, someone had to show us how to operate a saw before we cut our first piece of wood. Notice that I did not say you can find all the answers in a book or classroom. Education is just the warm up before the run.

Rebels Need An Extra Push

Okay, this is an engaging story for the personality types who can set internal goals and work towards them with little resistance. What about us rebels? We see people succeed, make plans to imitate them, and then unconsciously screw up our own agenda. We can't compel ourselves to listen to our instructions. We are our worst enemy.

My theory is that maybe you bought into your schemes consciously, but not emotionally. While you agree entirely with all the details, action plans, and conclusions of whatever story inspired you, something deep in your heart resists the most rational course of action possible.

I would imagine a broken bridge between your heart and your head remains that calls for an engineer. The hour has come for you to feel more passionate about your values than the discomfort & anxiety holding you back. You must unearth the reason why behind that prize you want to accomplish. Why do you want to start that business, audition for that show, go back to college, or get married? Why?

So what is your why? What is the purpose that awakens you, that subverts all impulses to self-sabotage? What is your reason for being that is stronger than your tendency to rebel against yourself? I am going to drum on about this like a child who is desperate for answers. For the sixth time, what is your WHY?

Your purpose for being has to shake your world like an earthquake awakens a city. Without a strong reason for moving forward, you may try to study, plan, and prepare, but forces more robust than you will overwhelm and squash all grand dreams.

We are as unshakable as earthquake-proof dwellings in our efforts to uncover the best options for our problems. Unlike the more delicate buildings that crumble from aftershocks, we won't build our lives on the most straightforward solutions if they fail to serve us. To really learn, marshall support, and make a lasting impact, you need to absorb the lesson by doing it yourself, and you can only do that if you feel strongly that this is the right course of action.

A person who can't trust their own mind disturbed by internal conflicts to remain the same should ideally be guided, not ordered, by a mentor or coach. Remember, if we try to think our way to the right solution, we will be relying on the same patterns of evidence that got us to this point. Did not Albert Einstein say, "We can't solve problems by using the same kind of thinking we used when we created them?"

Only A Strong Purpose Can Counteract A Force Of Nature Like Self-Sabotage

We must shut off the screaming, frightened part of our subconscious mind that blocks us from moving forward. If you are anything like me, that scary voice in your head needs to be muffled before you can feel your intuition rise up inside of you. Your genuine inner voice will thunder, "Why won't you listen to me? Why won't you go on an adventure to fulfill your purpose on this earth? When are you going to be the person your ancestors hoped you would be?"

I don't care if you are twenty, fifty, or eighty. You can rebuild a cracked fortress on solid ground after multiple life quakes. But it will get more challenging as you age. We develop the same patterns of behavior as we get older. Most people get up in the morning, use the washroom, make breakfast, get dressed, and leave the house in the same sequence and timing as they do every day. Maybe you have to break up your habits to succeed?

To disrupt such daily patterns of behavior is difficult, especially for rebels who resist change. It is human nature to stick with what works and rarely deviate from it. It's challenging to change a pattern once established.

Some achieve greatness only when they hit rock bottom, financially and emotionally, and their only way out is to push away all their mental barriers and go for it. Most of us are not in a desperate situation, so our motivation to change may not be strong enough. Perhaps we need to induce a crisis of your own making?

Winners are clear about what activities put them in the state of mind that makes them happy. Behind these activities is an overarching reason why they do what they do. With each little daily ritual, you form habits, habits become part of your identity, and you build momentum until it's hard to stop.

In my opinion, it's challenging for rebels to change their patterns of behaviors without the outside influence of other personality types. We dislike routines, mundane, and repetitive tasks because our minds have a low tolerance for boredom. Yet successful people swear that day to day trudging through the mud of work is the key to winning.

Therefore we must learn to cooperate with other personalities as supervisors, managers, or partners. Having people who hold us accountable for everyone's well-being in the organization is an ultimate leverage tool. When we share a common WHY there is the possibility that we can become unstoppable.

As her mentors showed her what to do during the Great Depression, suffragette Rose Schneiderman taught her followers to fight for working women's rights, continuing the leadership chain. Rose did not know if her advocacy for working women to gain the right to American social security would pay off. Still, Schneiderman had to tackle this injustice.

Labor organizer Schneiderman discovered her WHY after she observed inequality in the factories, houses, and inns of the United States. Rose would not settle until she helped improve wages and working conditions for waitresses, laundry workers, beauty parlor workers, and hotel maids.

If you struggle to get started, your actions must be so meaningful that you will cause others pain if you don't do what you said you would. For example, they would have to do further work to cover for you, go without food or shelter, or be forced to seek employment elsewhere.

When you convince yourself emotionally into being a shining example that others depend on, you are forced to conform to the greater good. You can resist your mind, but you cannot rebel against your soul. Quitting means letting down your own code of ethics as well as your aides. And that is a tough prize in the public arena to walk away from.

Challenge 18 - When you keep beating yourself up mentally for your past mistakes, you exhaust your emotional energy. Self-criticism is a way for the frightened subconscious to keep the thinker stuck in familiar patterns. Self-forgiveness is the path through to find your 'Why.'

Forgive yourself for your mistakes because you simply did know better. Forgive yourself because your mind can be released from old baggage and can start moving forward. Do it because you will feel better and your friends will notice that you seem more cheerful and energetic.

A person unburdened by the past has more strength than worriers to discover what they really want and more fortitude to push through a jungle of misinformation to become the person they aspire to be.

NOTES

CHAPTER 19

Sometimes All We Can Do Is
Remain Silent & Wait

I don't give a damn about standard conventions. Every human being has some inherent value. We are so busy rushing around consuming stuff we can only appreciate humans of beauty, economic means, and charm. What about everyone else? Not all rebels should, or can, fill their lives with action-oriented activities to fulfill their purpose. Breaking stride to perch and stare in wonder is an act of radicalism. We must resist becoming nothing more than 'human doings' instead of 'human beings.'

Maybe some rebels do not have to make noise, disrupt, innovate, and advocate for others because their energy is spent. Stages, like Covid-19, unemployment & recessions, fashion a request to activists to take a breather, rest, relax and even go on sabbaticals. Actually, all humans need to, with no exceptions, take mental breaks like vacations, naps, or meditations to give our minds a rest from stressful, hectic lives.

One mistake the ambitious make is they are trying to cram as many activities, work, and parties into their lives as possible. After all, don't you want to take as big a bite out of life as possible and have a rich collection of experiences to remember with satisfaction? Why not slow down a little bit so you can savor and enjoy the moments that matter the most? Beauty can't be appreciated when living in a blur.

The wealthy & professional classes, unrestrained by monetary worries, especially need to rebel against nonstop fun and embrace a little boredom. Quiet and rest is space where we unplug from our phones and televisions to think for a few moments about our problems and ask the universe for solutions. You must take a break from the hustle and bustle of existence to watch closely and ask who you really are, or life may pass you by.

Middle-class rebels are burdened by financial constraints and time poverty yet also enjoy the blessings of abundance. I propose that they also need some quiet time of solitude and reflection to make sense of what it means to be human. To rush through your days without taking daily breaks is to be thoughtless. Thoughtless materialists get run over by unfriendly organizations.

I urge you to drop activities that don't sustain contentment to make space for breathing. Are you so busy enjoying simple pleasures that you did not check to see if you were really happy or living your most tremendous potential? Please check your roadmap and see if you are going in the right direction.

It is tough to be satisfied when you are continuously broke, maxed out on credit cards, work long hours, and are one car repair from a financial disaster. Blue-collar workers on the margins have every right to sing the blues. At the risk of job loss or trouble with the law, individualists with empty pockets and family obligations can only fight silently by sustaining that fire of resistance within.

Financially struggling rebels may engage in limited activism and protest, but their primary purpose is to be enthusiastic and passionate for change, even if no evidence supports that belief. Feelings are shunned over results-oriented thought, but our decisions can be based on unsubstantiated fears, groupthink, and past experiences, limiting our choices and clarity of reason. We sometimes must sit in silence and call on our faith of brighter days.

Billions work in unimaginable conditions, twelve-hour days, hunched over machines or toiling in the fields. They can scratch out a living, making the difficult decision of which child goes to school or whether the medicine for illness will sustain more days than full bellies. Rebellion is a luxury ill-conceived because the powerless is easily replaceable.

Rebels can feel in their bones; something is wrong, but their feelings lack the language of words and don't have a clear voice like our thoughts. Impoverished revolutionaries only realize something is wrong when their bodies get tense, ill, stressed, or collapse from daily life.

We feel safe all over when we are growing, happy or loving, and physically terrible when we are sad, angry, jealous, or ill. Like those living in luxury, the masses in developing countries feel annoyed, bothered, or frustrated by their lot in life.

Rebels should not think about what they did in the past or will do in the future, and occupying days with endless tasks will not make these feelings go away. Sustaining a silent resistance in ones' heart may be appropriate under challenging times, for despondency brings with it boredom or depression that is guaranteed to hit like a ton of bricks.

Life is not the years, days, hours, and seconds we live in; it's a series of precious moments that we choose to cherish or squander. Nelson Mandela became a national symbol of strength and hope by resisting government pressure during twenty-seven years in prison. Inspired by Gandhi's ideas of non-violent resistance, Nelson Mandela fought for decades against the apartheid of South African's government.

I do not have easy answers for those in prison, working crushing hours, indebted for decades, or suffering under the tyranny of harsh parents. All you can do is endure, keep the faith, and hold on. Life does not permit all to raise their voice in protest. However, we can protect our name and our beliefs deep inside, no matter what happens to the shell that contains our heart.

We in the abundant West take for granted our liberties and access to abundance. Some rebels have no freedoms or even access to light, water, paper, and pen. Forget about the internet and books, their life is permanently darkened by ignorance and confusion. What remains is their emotions, intuitions, and moods. All have the opportunity to experience brief moments of joy and laughter, even if they are sex slaves, begging in the mud, or at death's door.

All those who live at the very bottom of society's well of tears can do is express their humanity by opening all doors to their emotions. Pay attention, rebels of all stripes. Find excuses to put yourself in a good mood, shut up your critical inner voice, and awaken those emotions that induce crying and laughing. Take advantage of your right attitude to have fun and be adventurous.

This respite of contentment is temporary so enjoy these brief pauses in short lifetimes. Your mind reawakens and is screaming that it is not happy. You might even become bored, frustrated, and angry while you live in this mood. Even as your nasty employers, your aging body, and mother nature war against you, you must resist. You may not be able to rebel against your circumstances, but you can recoil against misery and despair.

Challenge 19 - Ask people around you to give you reminders, rather than instructions, to do that thing you know you should do. We hate being pushed or guilt-tripped into doing unpleasant things. Instead, we need to relearn the benefits of completing the tasks and the downsides or consequences of avoidance.

Yes, this is another gratitude exercise. Can you see the benefits of doing unpleasant or dull jobs? By seeing the goodness of, say, sweeping the floor, you can appreciate the benefits as well - a clean floor means dirty air does not circulate into your face, hair, and lungs. What are the benefits of doing five distasteful tasks? By writing them down, hopefully, you will complete them expeditiously.

NOTES

CHAPTER 20

Self-Reflection Subverts A

Meaningless Life

If you have any fears, you desire success, and you know within your soul that you were born for a reason. You and I don't see that reason, but we are certain that we were meant to do great things.

Your fears mean you are unwittingly choosing a mediocre life over a view of abundance. I know you don't want to act this way. No one does. When you fight the natural progression of becoming who you were meant to be, you are literally burning your energy away until you run out of time.

We can't deal with death. None of us really believe we are going to have a gravestone covered with snow. Oh, logically, we understand the concept. Emotionally we refuse to believe it.

If we did, we would live life differently than how we really live. Robin Sharma tells the story of a man who asks an imaginary bird on his shoulder. "Is today the day I die? Have I lived my life to the fullest?" He does this each and every day to remind himself of his mortality.

Despite his past, Mr. Schindler knew risking his life for the powerless was the right thing to do. Oskar Schindler, a ruthless German industrialist and a member of the Nazi party, risked it all to rescue more than 1,000 Jews from deportation to Auschwitz during World War II.

Schindler saw that the Nazis progressed from cruel to sadistic in their treatment of the Polish Jews between 1939 and 1942. Despite a snowstorm of justifications, he realized he had no other choice but to help a thousand men, women, and children escape Europe. To do nothing would violate his code that forbade cowardice.

Mr. Schindler died in Germany, broke and virtually unknown, in 1974. Many of the people he helped and their descendants financed his body's transfer for burial in Israel, his final wish. His life story was revived by director Stephen Spielberg in the 1993 film Schindler's List. Very few people would say that this man's life was meaningless.

It's Not Meaningless If You Are Experiencing Enjoyable Things

I don't think people fear the end of their lives so much as they fear running out of time to do all the things that matter to them. The saddest group of people in the world think their life is as insignificant as melting snow. If anyone thinks this way, why even bother trying to become successful? Nothing makes your fears grow faster than the belief that life is pointless.

At the end of his life, a man who had fulfilling professions enjoyed his marriage, raised children, and had exciting adventures will likely have the right attitude towards the last phase of his life. Why fear death when he has done everything he wanted to do already?

A person who has been in bondage by his worries - fears learned through childhood experience - will never encounter the full richness of life. As his seasons spin to a halt, his mind will be full of regrets, of the friendships lost, the ample opportunities missed, the adventures never took.

Every child comes into life, expecting that he has unlimited potential to do or be whatever he wants to. Children have vivid imaginations and talk about that having experiences and jobs mature adults know to be unrealistic.

Have you noticed that the dreams and desires of children get smaller and smaller as they age? Is this a sign of maturity or indoctrination? Maybe we educate children out of their potential power even though we don't mean to do it. Nothing kills the spirit like being treated as nonentities of insignificance.

It is almost like forcing a plant to grow inside a small glass box. The plant that would naturally rise to its full potential can only grow to the size it's restricted to. We know we can be more than what we are, but the limiting beliefs of our talents, abilities, and strengths keep us small.

Most people have the strength to endure through most hardships. What the vast expanse of mortals lack is the belief that they can significantly impact their community and influence future generations.

Don't Focus On Meaningless Problems You Can't Solve

Apathy is the absence of activity. It's a defense mechanism that kicks in during survival mode thinking. Even when the snow melts and spring flowers bloom, most people don't drop the habit of apathy when winter hibernation is over. The warmth of the summer sun signifies the prospect of opportunity and progress. The only way to feel really alive is to become an active person, crackling with energy.

Awareness is the first step. You must actively manage your life and current beliefs in a way that is to your advantage. Just like an airplane can reach a completely different destination on a one-degree map adjustment, you can make a dramatic change in yourself by eliminating just this one primary belief: 'I can't handle it.'

Change this belief to 'I can do it,' 'I can survive any challenge' or "I am capable of my wildest heart's desires,' and you will be able to overcome your fear of success. Life is already hard enough, so why don't you drop this apathetic nihilism and be optimistic for a while? Try it out for a time.

Time is unfair. So why do we spend so much of our days grumbling about how cruel life is? Complaining about life's unfairness strengthens your mind's primary purpose to occupy your time with compulsive thoughts that take you nowhere.

Complaining and bickering with others feel like progress when, in reality, it takes you further from your goals. Instead of thinking of finding solutions, your mind uses energy to keep you living like a victim. You will avoid change, which is what your subconscious mind fears the most.

If you are complaining about your situation's unfairness, you ask someone else to make it fair for you. You are giving up your personal power as you moan about the state you are in. As you remember all the unfair things in your childhood, you will attract people and circumstances that maintain this victim identity.

Fight Back With Bigger Dreams

When you are not taking action towards what is really important, you are chronologically dying before your time, and the date you expire is just the final pronouncement.

But there is hope. For those who lost their way, decisions to live life to the fullest often comes following a period of suffering. Many successful people used a near-death experience or the death of a loved one as the spark to be fully alive.

To say life is meaningless is to stop living. To live an apathetic, meaningless life is to live a lie because you are lying to yourself that death is not coming. It makes death more significant because an empty life devoid of action will be filled with thoughts of regrets and dying unhappily.

If you walk the snow covered paths untread by others, you will become a distinguished person who understands how meaningful and adventurous life can be. Your goals will come alive, and your desire to become more than you are may overpower your fear of death.

Challenge 20 - Suggestions to Employ Gratitude:

- Be grateful that we can be successful without needing all the answers. Drop the certainty of being right and acknowledge that you might not have all the answers and never will.

- Be grateful you are not your thoughts. Your consciousness is part of you, a fractional part of your soul. Thinking doesn't always mean being.

- Don't chase the completion of your goals. Make chasing the dream so enjoyable that you become partly disappointed that you have arrived. Your life can be an exciting movie you don't want to forward to the end.

- Don't fight change. It's going to happen anyway—resistance causes unhappiness. Accepting change commands you forward the same way swimming with the current does. Be grateful for the chance because you get to experience a deeper variety of life.

- Blaming others and making yourself a victim temporarily feels good because it takes away the burden of responsibility. It also makes you mentally weak and reliant on the kindness of others. Be grateful you get to dominate your own life.

- Happiness is not the future. You must find it today. Be happy you can't postpone feeling contentment until you 'win" because you can choose to enjoy life right now.

- No one has all the answers. Only through connection and sharing with others will you get to your destination. No one is going to solve your problems but you. Be happy you can get help with encouragement and coaching from others.

- What you do matters. Your words matter. Your action matters. All your daily activities and conversations influence everyone around you and the friends, families, and people connected to the people you have impacted.

NOTES

CHAPTER 21

Faith before Flow

Time is such a strange thing. At the beginning of the work hour, it moves slowly as you struggle to build momentum in the face of tedious and boring tasks. Yet when the work hour draws to a close, you wonder where the time went? Whether you are content or miserable, life moves like a meandering stream, all the time in the world, until you get to an age where it becomes a raging river, so months feel like days and days like hours.

Many senior citizens look back on their youth and are happy with how it turned out. A far greater number view their past in regret. They mourn mostly their actions of neglect and selfishness. They regret not taking a chance and doing more things they wanted to do.

Rebels are in the greatest danger of joining the second group who failed to even try. We fight against others' expectations, and we fight against our own principles, which puts us back at square one.

There are so many things to advocate for - the environment, world peace, animal cruelty, workers' rights - and as voices of dissent, we want to use our power for good. We want to argue and change unfair rules to give others the opportunity for a better life. So why can't we? What is stopping us?

Get In The Zone To Get In The Flow

I believe the vast majority of us are not designing a work schedule that allows us to do our best work. We don't sit in a room quietly and think about problems until solutions present themselves. I recommend scheduling a few hours a day or week to turn off all distractions like phone calls, texts, social media, and emails and get to work.

If you want to be an agent of change, a river of knowledge, and a force for transformation, you need to work steadily and consistently. You must build a daily practice where you lose track of time and accomplish more in one hour than ordinary folks do in five.

Successful people are living in the present moment, specifically in a state of flow. Author Mihaly Csikszentmihalyi states, "Flow is the mental state of operation achieved when a person is fully engaged in what he or she is doing. It occurs when one is performing at his very best while immersed in a challenging task that demands intense concentration and commitment."

Imagine doing work or challenging & fun activities, and you enjoy it so much you forget about the time, people, and environment around you. You lose track of everything, yet you feel in control and absolutely charging towards your desired goals.

And it can only happen when your mind is not twisted in all directions by competing worries, thoughts, and memories. During flow, you lose all the self-monitoring and criticism because of the level of concentration required to maintain it.

Athletes talk about being 'in the zone' where they can score seemingly at will. Most jobs and tasks can put you in a state of mind inflow if you make it challenging enough. But you must like at least part of your work.

This is key. You must enjoy what you are doing; otherwise, your mind will try to escape the drudgery of work by replaying your old thoughts and slipping into daydreaming. If you like the task and find it challenging, you might become so absorbed that you can almost effortlessly race toward success.

Unpleasant Work Fill Up Unsatisfying Lives

Ironically, our subconscious minds are so full of limiting beliefs that many of us are not trying to find more challenging adventures. Unusual experiences lead to jobs where we may have more opportunities to get into the flow.

When our minds are full of negative thoughts and attitudes toward work, we won't even consider the possibility that work can be enjoyable. "Work is hard. Work is unpleasant. Only three hours till closing. Can't wait until retirement." Are they not thoughts that millions of people play in their heads every day?

Their co-workers and friends will also parrot these ideas, reinforcing the belief that you can only find happiness outside of work, and work is something you have to endure.

Have Faith Your Calling Is At Hand

In a world where negativity dominates our thinking, we have lost faith in our own abilities. Because if we, as adults, believed in ourselves the way we believed in ourselves as children, we all would have accomplished so much more than we have.

Faith is also seeing what has not yet been created. Some people have confidence in their religion but lack hope in life - their everyday experiences. This absence of conviction keeps them working with the expectation that no work exists where they can excel, progress, and savor.

Braille's inventor had some level of faith that his tactile writing and reading method would be used by the blind worldwide. Louis Braille was born with sight in 1809, but an eye injury left him blind at three. Studying at the Royal Institute for Blind Youth in Paris, Louis invented reading and writing for the blind involving raised dots, known as Braille.

By having faith, successful people took the chance and found their calling. This calling or purpose is made up of dozens or hundreds of daily activities, of which a few key ones are 'flow' actions. I believe Louis Braille spent many hours in a flow state, unaware of time passing, until his work was done.

If you have faith in yourself, you will see the possibilities of reaching the top of your profession or establishing good relationships with quality people even before it happens. You will believe in your success before there is any evidence that your dreams can come true.

Faith usually comes before flow, not before. If you don't believe, you will not even try. And if you don't try, you won't find those activities that are so enjoyable and challenging that you lose yourself in the present moment of progress.

We lack trust in our abilities to handle success as more significant than you and me. We believe we don't deserve it. Whenever we move towards success, we get anxious and find ways to procrastinate or sabotage ourselves to remind ourselves of who we think we are. But our chattering minds will continue to bother us, filling our consciousness with unpleasant thoughts all day and all night until we figure out how to shut it up.

Many of us resort to fun time-wasters like television, the internet, shopping, and excessive drinking. But these pleasures are only temporary and will not turn off that constant reminder in your mind: Why are you wasting time? You were meant for a better life than this!

Challenge 21 - Now that we are near the end, I challenge you to question and defy everything I wrote that does not feel proper to you. You are suspicious of everything, are you not? The book's entire purpose is to introduce you to your rebellious tendencies and ask you to try on appropriate concepts so you minimize struggle with any transformational identity shift.

If you were looking for explicit directions on your life's purpose, I am sorry; a short book rarely harbors those sorts of resolutions. Still, I hesitate to offer any advice without an extensive series of interviews to discover your specific details. Every person is unique, and counsel should be tailored to their needs in mind.

Have faith most of what is required is already hidden inside of you. Try something tiny, anything new, so you barely notice that first step forward. Do not dawdle, hesitate, halt, or cling to the familiar.

You must listen to the intuition that says YES, feelings that explode with enthusiasm, and convert elusive fantasies into heady realities.

Can you please write one line on your calendar of some critical purpose-driven task you can do? Better yet, select a partner and schedule a time, date, and place! Do this one thing, and who knows where it will take you. A book on philosophy has the sole purpose to reveal a new & distinct world to you. It's only through individual action that a world constructed in your mind, projected by an author, can leap off the pages and mature into your personal reality...

NOTES

ABOUT THE AUTHOR

James S. Zakaria is the author of Rebel, Untethered; Masterminds Are The Key; 48 Rules For Raging Against The World; and The Cry Of Bright Shadows. James lives in Toronto, Canada, and assists entrepreneurs & other organizations with writing growth-oriented Business Plan Summaries. Communicate with the author via email: JamesZakaria7@gmail.com

REFERENCES

Gretchen Rubin, 2017, The Four Tendencies, Harmony Books, NY (the following rebel characteristics are attributed to Ms. Rubin:

Rebels resist all expectations, inner & outer; 2. rebels want freedom, choice & self-expression; 3. they aren't persuaded by arguments; 4. they flout rules & conventions; 5. they like defying expectations; 6. they value authenticity & self-determination; 7. rebels are freer than they think; 8. rebels resist control & realize they are self-destructive; 9. they resist routines or repetitive tasks; 10.some rebels hate being rebels; 11. rebels respond to info, consequences & choice, not instruction; 12. they need to suffer adverse effects; 13. rebels frustrate themselves & others; 14. others should give rebels (freedom & choices); 15. paradoxical intervention helps: 16. Praise or reward can backfire; 17. Phraseology:You can't make me. Rules are made to be broken. You are not the boss of me; 18. Work in large institutions to rebel against)

Mark Manson, 2016, The Subtle Art of Not Giving a F*ck, HarperOne, New York

George S. Clason, 1988, The Richest Man In Babylon, Signet, New York

Og Mandino, 1983, The Greatest Salesman In The World, Bantam, New York

Robin Sharma, 1997, The Monk Who Sold His Ferrari, Harper Collins, New York

https://www.franklinboe.org/cms/lib/NJ01000817/Centricity/Domain/1362/BlackHistoryGreatMenandWomenWhoFoughtforFreedomforAfricanAmericans.pdf

https://www.summerboardingcourses.co.uk/blog/people-who-have-changed-the-world/

https://positivepsychology.com/mihaly-csikszentmihalyi-father-of-flow/

Gary John Bishop, 2016, Unf*ck Yourself, HarperOne, New York

Marie Forleo, 2019, Everything Is Figureoutable, Portfolio Penguin, New York

Jen Sincero, 2013, You Are A Badass, Running Press, Philadelphia

9 798859 164640